Serenity

Discover the Power of Inner Peace and Transform Your
Life: A Comprehensive Guide to Achieving Lasting Serenity
and Finding Fulfillment in the Chaos of Modern Life - From
Mindful Practices to Positive Habits, Learn to Overcome
Stress, Anxiety, and Negative Thoughts and Unlock Your
True Potential with the Ultimate Self-Help Resource

Lance P. Richards

Serenity: Discover the Power of Inner Peace and Transform Your Life: A Comprehensive Guide to Achieving Lasting Serenity and Finding Fulfillment in the Chaos of Modern Life - From Mindful Practices to Positive Habits, Learn to Overcome Stress, Anxiety, and Negative Thoughts and Unlock Your True Potential with the Ultimate Self-Help Resource

Table of Contents

01: The Importance of Serenity in Modern Life....................1

02: Understanding the Science of Inner Peace...................7

03: Exploring Different Forms of Meditation...................14

04: Developing Mindfulness for Everyday Life.................20

05: Mastering Breathing Techniques for Calmness............27

06: The Role of Yoga in Achieving Serenity.......................34

07: The Power of Positive Affirmations and Self-Talk........38

08: Navigating Negative Thoughts and Emotions.............43

09: Overcoming Anxiety with Cognitive Behavioral Therapy
....47

10: Strategies for Coping with Stress and Burnout............51

11: The Connection between Sleep and Inner Peace...........58

12: The Benefits of a Healthy Diet for Serenity...................64

13: The Impact of Exercise on Mental Well-being..............70

14: Cultivating Gratitude and Appreciation........................76

15: Forgiveness and Letting Go of Resentment..................80

16: The Importance of Self-Care in Achieving Serenity......84

17: Finding Purpose and Meaning in Life...........................88

18: Pursuing Personal Growth and Development..............92

19: The Role of Relationships in Inner Peace...................100

20: Setting Boundaries and Learning to Say No...............107

21: Nurturing a Supportive Network.................................113

22: Building Resilience and Coping Skills.........................119

23: Cultivating a Positive Mindset....................................125

24: Embracing Change and Uncertainty............................129

25: Letting Go of Perfectionism and Embracing Imperfection..132

26: Tapping into Your Inner Strength and Courage.........138

27: Overcoming Fears and Limiting Beliefs.....................144

28: Discovering Your Values and Priorities.....................150

29: Setting Goals for a Fulfilling Life..............................153

30: Strategies for Time Management and Productivity....158

31: Balancing Work and Life for Inner Peace...................162

32: The Power of Gratitude and Giving Back...................169

33: Incorporating Serenity into Your Daily Routine.........172

34: Overcoming Obstacles and Challenges......................178

35: Celebrating Your Progress and Successes...................186

36: Embracing a Life of Serenity and Fulfillment.............192

Thank You...199

Disclaimer...200

01: The Importance of Serenity in Modern Life

The modern world is a fast-paced, high-pressure environment. We are constantly bombarded with information, demands, and expectations from all angles, whether it's work, family, or social media. We are expected to be productive, successful, and happy all the time, even when we are facing difficult challenges or setbacks.

It's no wonder that stress, anxiety, and burnout have become such prevalent issues in today's society. Many of us struggle to find a sense of peace and contentment in our lives, even when everything seems to be going well. We are constantly chasing after the next big thing, trying to keep up with the latest trends and technologies, and striving to achieve more and more every day.

But what if we could find a way to break free from this cycle of stress and discontentment? What if we could learn to cultivate a sense of inner peace and serenity, even in the midst of chaos and uncertainty? This is the power of contentment, and it's something that anyone can achieve with the right tools and mindset.

01: THE IMPORTANCE OF SERENITY IN MODERN LIFE

In this chapter, we will explore the importance of serenity in modern life, and why it's essential for our mental, emotional, and physical wellbeing. We will also discuss some practical strategies and tips for achieving lasting serenity and contentment, even in the midst of the most challenging situations.

The Benefits of Serenity

Serenity is not just a pleasant feeling or a temporary state of mind. It's a powerful tool for achieving lasting happiness, fulfillment, and success in all areas of life. Here are just a few of the many benefits of cultivating serenity in your daily life:

Reduced Stress and Anxiety: When we are in a state of serenity, we are less likely to be affected by external stressors and triggers. We are able to stay calm, centered, and focused, even in the midst of difficult situations. This can lead to reduced levels of stress and anxiety, which can have a positive impact on our physical and mental health.

Improved Mental Clarity and Focus: Serenity allows us to quiet our minds and focus on the present moment. This can lead to improved mental clarity, concentration, and focus, which can be beneficial for work, school, or any other task that requires sustained attention.

Increased Creativity and Productivity: When we are in a state of serenity, we are more open to new ideas and insights. This can lead to increased creativity and productivity, as we are able to think outside the box and find innovative solutions to problems.

Improved Relationships and Communication: Serenity can also help us to communicate more effectively with others, as we are less likely to be reactive or defensive in our interactions. This can lead to improved relationships, both at work and in our personal lives.

Greater Sense of Fulfillment and Purpose: When we are able to find a sense of serenity and contentment in our lives, we are more likely to feel fulfilled and purposeful. We are able to appreciate the small moments of joy and beauty in our lives, and to find meaning in our work and relationships.

Strategies for Achieving Serenity

So how can we cultivate serenity in our daily lives? Here are some practical strategies and tips for achieving lasting peace and contentment, no matter what challenges we may face:

Practice Mindfulness: Mindfulness is the practice of being present and aware in the current moment, without judgment or distraction. It can help us to stay grounded and centered, even in the midst of chaos and stress. Try incorporating mindfulness into your daily routine by setting aside a few minutes each day to meditate, breathe deeply, or simply focus on your senses and surroundings.

Cultivate Positive Habits: Positive habits such as exercise, healthy eating, and getting enough sleep can have a significant impact on our mental and physical wellbeing. When we take care of our bodies, we are better equipped to handle stress and challenges. Try to establish a regular exercise routine, eat a balanced diet, and prioritize getting enough sleep each night.

Set Realistic Expectations: One of the main sources of stress and anxiety in modern life is the pressure to constantly achieve more and do better. While it's important to have goals and aspirations, it's also important to set realistic expectations for ourselves. Don't expect perfection or success overnight – instead, focus on making small, achievable progress each day.

Practice Gratitude: Gratitude is the practice of focusing on the positive aspects of our lives and being thankful for them. When we cultivate a sense of gratitude, we are more likely to find joy and contentment in our daily experiences. Try keeping a gratitude journal or simply take a few minutes each day to reflect on the things you are thankful for.

Embrace Mindful Technology Use: Technology can be both a blessing and a curse when it comes to cultivating serenity. On the one hand, it can provide us with valuable tools for managing stress and staying connected to loved ones. On the other hand, it can also be a major source of distraction and overwhelm. Try to establish mindful technology use habits, such as setting boundaries on social media, turning off notifications during certain times of the day, and using technology intentionally rather than compulsively.

Find a Support System: Cultivating serenity is not something that we can do alone. It's important to have a support system of friends, family, or professionals who can help us navigate the ups and downs of life. Don't be afraid to reach out for help when you need it, whether it's through therapy, support groups, or simply talking to a trusted friend.

In conclusion, cultivating serenity is essential for achieving lasting happiness, fulfillment, and success in modern life. By practicing mindfulness, cultivating positive habits, setting realistic expectations, practicing gratitude, embracing mindful technology use, and finding a support system, we can all learn to overcome stress, anxiety, and negative thoughts and unlock our true potential for inner peace and contentment. So take a deep breath, let go of your worries, and embrace the power of serenity in your life today.

02: Understanding the Science of Inner Peace

Introduction

The world we live in is fast-paced, chaotic, and often stressful. We constantly feel the pressure to perform, succeed, and keep up with the expectations of society. In this environment, it can be difficult to find inner peace and contentment. However, inner peace is not an elusive concept; it is something that we can cultivate and develop within ourselves. In this chapter, we will explore the science of inner peace and understand the mechanisms behind it.

What is Inner Peace?

Inner peace is a state of mind that is characterized by calmness, tranquility, and a sense of contentment. It is the absence of inner turmoil, negative thoughts, and emotions. When we are at peace with ourselves, we are able to handle stress and challenges with greater resilience and ease. We are able to make decisions from a place of clarity and wisdom, rather than being influenced by our emotions.

Why is Inner Peace Important?

Inner peace is important because it is the foundation for our mental, emotional, and physical well-being. When we are at peace, we are able to think more clearly, focus better, and make better decisions. We are also able to handle stress and challenges with greater resilience, which reduces the risk of stress-related health problems such as hypertension, diabetes, and heart disease.

The Science of Inner Peace

The science of inner peace is a relatively new field of research, but it has already yielded some interesting findings. Here are some of the key discoveries:

The Brain Changes During Meditation

Studies have shown that regular meditation can change the structure and function of the brain. Specifically, meditation has been shown to increase the thickness of the prefrontal cortex, the part of the brain that is responsible for decision-making, attention, and self-awareness. Meditation has also been shown to reduce activity in the amygdala, the part of the brain that is responsible for processing emotions such as fear and anxiety.

02: UNDERSTANDING THE SCIENCE OF INNER PEACE

Mindfulness Reduces Stress

Mindfulness is the practice of being present in the moment and non-judgmentally observing our thoughts and emotions. Studies have shown that mindfulness can reduce stress and anxiety. One study found that people who practiced mindfulness for eight weeks had reduced activity in the amygdala, the part of the brain that is responsible for processing emotions such as fear and anxiety.

Positive Thinking Changes the Brain

Studies have shown that positive thinking can change the brain in positive ways. When we think positively, our brains release neurotransmitters such as dopamine and serotonin, which are associated with feelings of happiness and well-being. Positive thinking has also been shown to increase activity in the prefrontal cortex, the part of the brain that is responsible for decision-making, attention, and self-awareness.

Gratitude Boosts Happiness

Gratitude is the practice of focusing on the things we are grateful for. Studies have shown that gratitude can boost happiness and well-being. One study found that people who kept a gratitude journal for two weeks had increased activity in the prefrontal cortex, the part of the brain that is responsible for decision-making, attention, and self-awareness.

Compassion Reduces Negative Emotions

Compassion is the practice of showing kindness and empathy towards ourselves and others. Studies have shown that compassion can reduce negative emotions such as anger, anxiety, and depression. One study found that people who practiced compassion meditation had reduced activity in the amygdala, the part of the brain that is responsible for processing emotions such as fear and anxiety.

How to Cultivate Inner Peace

Now that we understand the science of inner peace, let's explore some practical ways to cultivate it:

Practice Meditation

Meditation is one of the most effective ways to cultivate inner peace. Find a quiet place, sit comfortably, and focus on your breath.

When thoughts arise, simply observe them without judgment and return your focus to your breath. Start with just a few minutes each day and gradually increase the duration as you become more comfortable with the practice.

Practice Mindfulness

Mindfulness involves being present in the moment and non-judgmentally observing our thoughts and emotions. Practice mindfulness by paying attention to your surroundings and focusing on your senses. When you notice your mind wandering, gently bring your focus back to the present moment.

Cultivate Positive Thinking

Practice positive thinking by focusing on the positive aspects of your life and reframing negative thoughts into positive ones. For example, instead of thinking "I can't do this," reframe it to "I can do this with effort and practice." Focus on your strengths and accomplishments rather than your weaknesses and failures.

Practice Gratitude

Gratitude involves focusing on the things we are grateful for. Keep a gratitude journal and write down three things you are grateful for each day. Take time to appreciate the people and things in your life and express gratitude to those who have made a positive impact on you.

Practice Compassion

Compassion involves showing kindness and empathy towards ourselves and others. Practice compassion by treating yourself with kindness and self-care. Be patient with yourself and acknowledge your strengths and limitations. Show kindness and empathy towards others by listening actively and offering support.

Conclusion

In conclusion, cultivating inner peace is an essential component of our overall well-being. Understanding the science of inner peace can help us develop practical strategies to cultivate it in our lives. By practicing meditation, mindfulness, positive thinking, gratitude, and compassion, we can transform our lives and find lasting serenity and content-

02: UNDERSTANDING THE SCIENCE OF INNER PEACE

ment in the chaos of modern life.

03: Exploring Different Forms of Meditation

Meditation has been practiced for thousands of years by people all over the world. It is an ancient practice that involves training the mind to focus and be present in the moment. There are many different forms of meditation, each with its own unique benefits and techniques. In this chapter, we will explore some of the most popular forms of meditation, their benefits, and how to practice them.

Mindfulness Meditation

Mindfulness meditation is one of the most popular forms of meditation. It involves focusing your attention on the present moment and being aware of your thoughts, feelings, and sensations without judgment. This form of meditation has been shown to reduce stress, improve focus and concentration, and increase feelings of well-being.

To practice mindfulness meditation, find a quiet place where you won't be disturbed. Sit comfortably with your back straight and your eyes closed. Focus your attention on your breath, noticing the sensations of each inhale and exhale. When your mind wanders, gently bring your attention back to your breath.

Transcendental Meditation

Transcendental Meditation (TM) is a form of meditation that involves repeating a mantra, which is a word or phrase that is repeated silently in the mind. This form of meditation is said to help quiet the mind and promote relaxation.

To practice TM, find a quiet place where you won't be disturbed. Sit comfortably with your back straight and your eyes closed. Choose a mantra that has personal meaning to you, and repeat it silently in your mind. When your mind wanders, gently bring your attention back to the mantra.

Loving-Kindness Meditation

Loving-kindness meditation, also known as Metta meditation, is a form of meditation that involves cultivating feelings of love and compassion towards oneself and others. This form of meditation is said to increase feelings of happiness and reduce feelings of anxiety and depression.

To practice loving-kindness meditation, find a quiet place where you won't be disturbed. Sit comfortably with your back straight and your eyes closed. Begin by focusing on yourself and repeating the phrase, "May I be happy, may I be healthy, may I be safe, may I be at peace." Then, extend these feelings of love and compassion to others, starting with a loved one, then a neutral person, and finally to someone you have difficulty with.

Yoga Meditation

Yoga meditation is a form of meditation that is practiced as part of a yoga practice. It involves focusing the mind on the breath while holding different yoga poses. This form of meditation is said to improve flexibility, reduce stress, and increase feelings of well-being.

To practice yoga meditation, find a quiet place where you won't be disturbed. Begin by practicing some yoga poses to warm up the body. Then, focus your attention on your breath while holding each pose. When your mind wanders, gently bring your attention back to your breath.

Walking Meditation

Walking meditation is a form of meditation that involves walking slowly and mindfully while focusing on the sensations of the body and the environment around you. This form of meditation is said to improve focus, reduce stress, and increase feelings of well-being.

To practice walking meditation, find a quiet place where you can walk without distractions. Begin by standing still and taking a few deep breaths. Then, start walking slowly, focusing your attention on the sensations of your feet touching the ground and the movement of your body. When your mind wanders, gently bring your attention back to your body and the environment around you.

Body Scan Meditation

Body scan meditation is a form of meditation that involves focusing your attention on different parts of your body, one at a time, and noticing any sensations or feelings that arise. This form of meditation is said to increase awareness of the body and reduce feelings of stress and tension.

To practice body scan meditation, find a quiet place where you won't be disturbed. Lie down comfortably on your back with your arms at your sides and your eyes closed. Begin by focusing your attention on your breath, noticing the sensations of each inhale and exhale. Then, slowly move your attention through each part of your body, starting at your toes and moving up to your head. Notice any sensations or feelings that arise, without judgment. When your mind wanders, gently bring your attention back to the body part you are focusing on.

Visualization Meditation

Visualization meditation is a form of meditation that involves using the imagination to create a mental image of a peaceful or positive scene. This form of meditation is said to reduce stress and increase feelings of relaxation and wellbeing.

To practice visualization meditation, find a quiet place where you won't be disturbed. Sit comfortably with your back straight and your eyes closed. Imagine a peaceful scene, such as a beach or a forest. Use all of your senses to create a vivid mental image of the scene, including the sounds, smells, and textures. Stay with the scene for as long as you like, allowing yourself to feel a sense of peace and relaxation.

Chakra Meditation

Chakra meditation is a form of meditation that focuses on the seven chakras, which are energy centers located in the body. This form of meditation is said to balance the chakras and promote physical, emotional, and spiritual healing.

To practice chakra meditation, find a quiet place where you won't be disturbed. Sit comfortably with your back straight and your eyes closed. Focus your attention on each of the seven chakras, starting at the base of the spine and moving up to the crown of the head. Imagine each chakra as a spinning wheel of energy, and visualize the color associated with each chakra. Stay with each chakra for a few moments, allowing yourself to feel a sense of balance and harmony.

In conclusion, there are many different forms of meditation, each with its own unique benefits and techniques. Whether you are new to meditation or an experienced practitioner, there is a form of meditation that can help you find inner peace and transform your life. Experiment with different forms of meditation to find the one that works best for you, and make a daily practice a part of your routine. With patience and dedication, you can experience the transformative power of meditation and achieve lasting serenity and contentment in the chaos of modern life.

04: Developing Mindfulness for Everyday Life

Introduction

In our modern world, we are constantly bombarded with distractions, stressors, and negative thoughts that can hinder our ability to find peace and contentment. But, amidst the chaos, it is possible to find serenity and develop mindfulness for everyday life.

Mindfulness is the practice of being present and aware of our thoughts, feelings, and surroundings without judgment. It is a powerful tool that can help us reduce stress, manage anxiety, and find inner peace.

In this chapter, we will explore the benefits of mindfulness and provide practical tips and techniques to develop mindfulness in our everyday lives.

The Benefits of Mindfulness

Mindfulness has numerous benefits that can positively impact our physical, mental, and emotional well-being. Here are some of the most significant benefits of mindfulness:

Reduced Stress: Mindfulness can help reduce stress by increasing our awareness of our thoughts and emotions. By recognizing our stress triggers, we can respond to them more effectively and reduce their impact on our lives.

Improved Emotional Regulation: Mindfulness can help us regulate our emotions by increasing our awareness of them. This allows us to respond to our emotions in a healthy and productive way, rather than reacting impulsively.

Enhanced Focus and Concentration: Mindfulness can improve our ability to focus and concentrate by training our minds to stay present in the moment.

Increased Compassion and Empathy: Mindfulness can help us cultivate compassion and empathy for ourselves and others. By practicing non-judgment and acceptance, we can develop a deeper understanding of our own emotions and the emotions of others.

Improved Sleep: Mindfulness can improve the quality of our sleep by reducing racing thoughts and anxiety.

Practical Tips for Developing Mindfulness

Now that we understand the benefits of mindfulness, let's explore some practical tips for developing mindfulness in our everyday lives:

Start Small: Developing mindfulness takes time and practice, so start with small steps. Set aside a few minutes each day to focus on your breath and observe your thoughts and feelings without judgment.

Practice Mindful Breathing: Mindful breathing is a simple yet powerful technique for developing mindfulness. Focus on your breath and observe the sensation of air flowing in and out of your body.

Use Mindful Reminders: Use reminders to bring yourself back to the present moment throughout the day. This can be as simple as setting an alarm or using a sticky note with a mindfulness message.

Practice Mindful Eating: Mindful eating is a great way to practice mindfulness and improve your relationship with food. Take time to savor each bite and observe the taste, texture, and sensation of the food.

Engage Your Senses: Engaging your senses can help you

stay present in the moment. Take a few minutes each day to observe your surroundings, noticing the colors, sounds, and smells around you.

Practice Gratitude: Practicing gratitude can help you cultivate a positive mindset and improve your overall well-being. Take time each day to reflect on the things you are grateful for.

Use Guided Meditations: Guided meditations are a great way to develop mindfulness and reduce stress. There are many free resources available online, such as apps and YouTube videos.

Find a Mindfulness Buddy: Finding a mindfulness buddy can help you stay accountable and motivated in your mindfulness practice. You can support each other and share tips and techniques.

Incorporating Mindfulness into Your Daily Routine

Incorporating mindfulness into your daily routine can be a powerful way to reduce stress and improve your overall well-being. Here are some tips for incorporating mindfulness into your daily routine:

Start Your Day Mindfully: Begin your day with a few minutes of mindful breathing or reflection. This can set a positive tone for the rest of your day.

Take Mindful Breaks: Take short breaks throughout the day to practice mindfulness. This can be as simple as taking a few deep breaths or going for a short walk.

Practice Mindful Movement: Incorporate mindful movement into your daily routine, such as yoga or tai chi. These practices can help you stay present in the moment and improve your physical well-being.

Use Mindful Technology: Use technology to support your mindfulness practice, such as apps or reminders. However, be mindful of the impact technology can have on your well-being and limit your screen time.

Practice Mindful Communication: Practice active listening and non-judgmental communication with others. This can improve your relationships and reduce stress.

End Your Day Mindfully: End your day with a few minutes of reflection or gratitude. This can help you unwind and prepare for a restful night's sleep.

04: DEVELOPING MINDFULNESS FOR EVERYDAY LIFE

Challenges in Developing Mindfulness

Developing mindfulness can be challenging, especially in our fast-paced and distracted world. Here are some common challenges and how to overcome them:

Busy Mind: Our minds can often be filled with racing thoughts, making it difficult to stay present. To overcome this, simply observe your thoughts without judgment and bring your focus back to your breath.

Time Constraints: Finding time for mindfulness can be challenging, but even a few minutes a day can make a difference. Prioritize your well-being and make time for mindfulness in your daily routine.

Consistency: Consistency is key in developing mindfulness. Set a regular time and place for your mindfulness practice and stick to it as much as possible.

Distractions: Our modern world is full of distractions, but mindfulness can help us stay present amidst them. Use reminders and mindful techniques to bring yourself back to the present moment.

Conclusion

Developing mindfulness for everyday life can be a powerful way to reduce stress, improve emotional regulation, and find inner peace. By incorporating mindfulness into our daily routines and overcoming common challenges, we can cultivate a more fulfilling and content life.

Remember, developing mindfulness takes time and practice, so be patient and kind to yourself. With commitment and dedication, you can unlock the power of mindfulness and transform your life.

05: Mastering Breathing Techniques for Calmness

In today's fast-paced world, it can be easy to feel overwhelmed and stressed out. From the constant barrage of emails and notifications to the demands of work and personal life, it can sometimes feel like we're being pulled in a million different directions.

But amidst all this chaos, there is a simple yet powerful tool that can help us find peace and tranquility: our breath. Breathing is something we do all day, every day, yet few of us pay attention to it. By learning to control our breathing, we can tap into a deep well of inner calm and find a sense of contentment that can carry us through even the most challenging of times.

In this chapter, we'll explore the art of mastering breathing techniques for calmness. From deep breathing to mindfulness meditation, we'll examine a variety of practices that can help you achieve a greater sense of serenity and fulfillment in your life.

The Science of Breathing

05: MASTERING BREATHING TECHNIQUES FOR CALMNESS

Before we dive into the techniques themselves, let's take a moment to explore the science behind breathing. When we breathe in, our body takes in oxygen, which is then transported to our cells to be used for energy. When we breathe out, we release carbon dioxide, which is a waste product that our body needs to get rid of.

But breathing isn't just about the exchange of gases - it's also intricately tied to our nervous system. When we breathe deeply and slowly, we activate our parasympathetic nervous system, which is responsible for the "rest and digest" response. This is the opposite of the sympathetic nervous system, which is activated when we're stressed or anxious and triggers the "fight or flight" response.

So by controlling our breathing, we can actually shift our body into a more relaxed state, which can help us feel calmer, more focused, and less reactive to stress.

Breathing Techniques for Calmness

Now that we understand the science behind breathing, let's explore some of the techniques that can help us tap into that deep well of inner calm. Remember, these techniques are not one-size-fits-all - everyone's body and mind are different, so it's important to experiment and find what works best for you.

Deep Breathing

The simplest and most straightforward technique for calming the mind and body is deep breathing. This involves taking slow, deliberate breaths in through the nose and out through the mouth, focusing on filling your lungs completely with air and then slowly releasing it.

To practice deep breathing, find a comfortable seated or lying position and close your eyes. Place your hands on your belly and inhale deeply, feeling your abdomen expand as you fill your lungs with air. Hold the breath for a few seconds, then exhale slowly, feeling your belly deflate as you release the air. Repeat this process for a few minutes, focusing on the sensation of your breath moving in and out of your body.

Box Breathing

Another technique that can help you achieve a greater sense

of calm is box breathing. This technique involves inhaling for a set count, holding the breath for the same count, exhaling for the same count, and then holding the breath again for the same count.

To practice box breathing, find a comfortable seated position and close your eyes. Inhale deeply for a count of four, hold the breath for a count of four, exhale slowly for a count of four, and then hold the breath again for a count of four. Repeat this process for a few minutes, focusing on the rhythm of your breath and the sensation of calm that it brings.

Alternate Nostril Breathing

A more advanced technique for calming the mind and body is alternate nostril breathing, also known as Nadi Shodhana. This technique involves using the fingers to alternate between blocking one nostril and breathing through the other, which can help balance the flow of energy throughout the body and promote a greater sense of harmony and calmness.

To practice alternate nostril breathing, sit in a comfortable position and use your right hand to place your thumb on your right nostril and your ring finger on your left nostril. Inhale deeply through your left nostril, then use your ring finger to close it and exhale through your right nostril. Inhale through your right nostril, then use your thumb to close it and exhale through your left nostril. Continue this process, alternating nostrils with each inhale and exhale, for a few minutes.

Mindful Breathing Meditation

In addition to these specific breathing techniques, mindfulness meditation can also be a powerful tool for achieving inner peace and contentment. This practice involves focusing your attention on your breath and observing your thoughts and feelings without judgment.

To practice mindful breathing meditation, find a quiet and comfortable space and sit in a relaxed position. Close your eyes and focus on the sensation of your breath moving in and out of your body. When your mind wanders, gently bring your attention back to your breath, without getting caught up in your thoughts or emotions. Practice this for a few minutes, gradually increasing the amount of time you

spend meditating as you become more comfortable with the
practice.

Incorporating Breathing Techniques into Your Daily Life

Now that you've learned some powerful breathing techniques for calmness, the next step is to incorporate them
into your daily life. Here are some tips for doing so:

Set aside time each day for breathing exercises or meditation. This could be first thing in the morning, during your
lunch break, or before bed.

Find a quiet and comfortable space where you can practice
without distractions. This could be a dedicated meditation
room, a quiet corner of your home, or even a park or out-
door space.

Use breathing techniques to calm your mind and body in
stressful situations. When you feel overwhelmed or anxious,
take a few deep breaths or try one of the other techniques
we've discussed to help bring you back to a state of
calmness and balance.

Practice gratitude and positive self-talk as you breathe. As you inhale, think of something you're grateful for or a positive affirmation. As you exhale, release any negative thoughts or emotions.

Remember that mastering breathing techniques takes time and practice. Don't get discouraged if you don't feel immediate results - keep at it, and you'll begin to notice a greater sense of calm and contentment in your life.

Conclusion

Mastering breathing techniques for calmness can be a powerful tool for finding inner peace and contentment in the chaos of modern life. Whether you're practicing deep breathing, box breathing, alternate nostril breathing, or mindful meditation, these techniques can help you tap into a deep well of inner calm and find a sense of fulfillment and purpose in your life. So take a few minutes each day to focus on your breath, and discover the transformative power of inner peace.

06: The Role of Yoga in Achieving Serenity

In today's world, the importance of maintaining physical and mental wellbeing has never been more evident. With the hustle and bustle of modern life, it's easy to get swept up in the chaos and lose sight of what truly matters. Finding inner peace and contentment is a constant struggle, but it's one that can be achieved with the help of a consistent yoga practice.

Yoga has been practiced for centuries and has been proven to have numerous health benefits. Beyond its physical benefits, yoga is a practice that can help individuals find calmness and clarity in their minds. Through the combination of mindful movements and conscious breathing, yoga helps practitioners tune out the noise of daily life and tap into their inner selves.

One of the key benefits of yoga is its ability to help individuals reduce stress and anxiety. In today's world, stress has become a part of everyday life, and it can take a toll on our mental and physical health. Regular yoga practice has been shown to reduce cortisol levels in the body, which is the hormone associated with stress. The physical practice of yoga helps individuals release tension and reduce muscle stiffness, which can also help with stress reduction.

Beyond stress reduction, yoga can also help with anxiety. In yoga, the breath is emphasized as an important tool for calming the mind. Conscious breathing techniques help practitioners slow down their breathing, which in turn slows down their heart rate and reduces feelings of anxiety. The physical movements in yoga also help individuals become more aware of their bodies and their physical sensations, which can help them better identify and manage their emotions.

Another benefit of yoga is its ability to improve sleep quality. A consistent yoga practice has been shown to improve sleep quality and help individuals fall asleep faster. The relaxation and stress-reducing benefits of yoga can also help individuals who suffer from insomnia or other sleep disorders.

Yoga can also be an effective tool for individuals looking to improve their overall mental health. In addition to reducing stress and anxiety, regular yoga practice has been shown to improve symptoms of depression. The mindfulness and awareness that comes with yoga can help individuals better manage their negative thoughts and emotions.

For those looking to achieve contentment and serenity in their lives, yoga can be an essential tool. By helping individuals tune out the noise of daily life and focus on their inner selves, yoga can help individuals find a sense of calmness and clarity. A consistent yoga practice can help individuals cultivate a deeper understanding of themselves, their emotions, and their bodies.

In addition to the physical and mental benefits of yoga, there is also a sense of community that comes with practicing yoga. Many yoga studios offer classes for practitioners of all levels, and there is often a sense of camaraderie and support among the students. This sense of community can be especially helpful for individuals who may be struggling with feelings of isolation or loneliness.

In conclusion, the role of yoga in achieving serenity and contentment cannot be overstated. Regular yoga practice has numerous physical and mental health benefits, including reducing stress and anxiety, improving sleep quality, and improving symptoms of depression. Through the combination of mindful movements and conscious breathing, yoga helps individuals tune out the noise of daily life and tap into their inner selves. Whether you're a seasoned practitioner or a beginner, incorporating yoga into your daily routine can help you achieve lasting serenity and find fulfillment in the chaos of modern life.

07: The Power of Positive Affirmations and Self-Talk

In today's world, it's hard to find a moment of peace and quiet. With the constant barrage of information and stimuli, it's easy to get lost in the chaos of everyday life. But amidst all the noise and distractions, there is a powerful tool that can help us find the inner peace we so desperately crave: positive affirmations and self-talk.

Positive affirmations and self-talk are powerful tools for transforming your mindset and unlocking your true potential. By consciously replacing negative self-talk with positive affirmations, you can shift your mindset from one of doubt and self-criticism to one of confidence and self-love. In this chapter, we'll explore the science behind positive affirmations and self-talk and provide practical tips for incorporating these powerful tools into your daily routine.

Understanding Positive Affirmations and Self-Talk

At their core, positive affirmations and self-talk are simply statements that affirm positive qualities and beliefs about yourself. These statements can be general, such as "I am worthy of love and respect," or specific, such as "I am capable of achieving my goals." The key is to make these statements in the present tense and to phrase them positively. For example, instead of saying "I am not a failure," you might say "I am successful in all that I do."

The science behind positive affirmations and self-talk is rooted in the concept of neuroplasticity. Essentially, this means that our brains are malleable and can be rewired through repeated thoughts and behaviors. When we consistently repeat positive affirmations and engage in positive self-talk, we create new neural pathways that reinforce positive beliefs about ourselves. This, in turn, can lead to a more positive outlook on life, increased self-confidence, and improved mental health.

Practical Tips for Incorporating Positive Affirmations and Self-Talk into Your Daily Routine

Start with a few simple affirmations: If you're new to positive affirmations and self-talk, start with a few simple statements that resonate with you. Write them down and repeat them to yourself throughout the day. Over time, you can add more affirmations to your repertoire.

07: THE POWER OF POSITIVE AFFIRMATIONS AND SELF-TALK

Make it a daily habit: Consistency is key when it comes to positive affirmations and self-talk. Try to set aside a few minutes each day to focus on your affirmations. Whether you do this in the morning, during your lunch break, or before bed, make it a non-negotiable part of your daily routine.

Use visualization: Visualization is a powerful tool for reinforcing positive affirmations. As you repeat your affirmations, imagine yourself embodying those qualities and achieving your goals. This can help solidify those beliefs in your mind and make them feel more real.

Mix it up: Don't be afraid to switch up your affirmations from time to time. As you grow and evolve, your affirmations may change as well. Experiment with different statements and see what resonates with you at different points in your life.

Practice self-compassion: Positive affirmations and self-talk are not a magic solution for all of life's problems. It's important to practice self-compassion and acknowledge that there will be times when you struggle. When this happens, be kind to yourself and remember that it's all part of the journey.

The Benefits of Positive Affirmations and Self-Talk

There are countless benefits to incorporating positive affirmations and self-talk into your daily routine. Here are just a few:

Increased self-confidence: By repeating positive affirmations and engaging in positive self-talk, you can build up your sense of self-worth and confidence.

Reduced stress and anxiety: Focusing on positive affirmations can help shift your mindset away from negative thoughts and reduce feelings of stress and anxiety.

Improved mental health: Consistently engaging in positive self-talk can lead to improved mental health outcomes, such as reduced symptoms of depression and improved overall well-being.

Greater resilience: When faced with challenges or setbacks, positive affirmations and self-talk can help you bounce back and stay motivated.

07: THE POWER OF POSITIVE AFFIRMATIONS AND SELF-TALK

Improved relationships: By cultivating a positive mindset and sense of self-worth, you may find that your relationships with others improve as well.

Final Thoughts

Positive affirmations and self-talk are powerful tools for transforming your mindset and unlocking your true potential. By incorporating these practices into your daily routine, you can cultivate a more positive outlook on life, improve your mental health, and achieve greater success in all areas of your life.

Remember, consistency is key when it comes to positive affirmations and self-talk. Make it a non-negotiable part of your daily routine and be patient with yourself as you work to build new neural pathways and shift your mindset. With time and practice, you'll find that positive affirmations and self-talk become second nature, and you'll reap the many benefits that come with a positive mindset and sense of self-worth.

08: Navigating Negative Thoughts and Emotions

Introduction

Negative thoughts and emotions are an inevitable part of human experience. Even the most positive and optimistic individuals encounter negative emotions at some point in their lives. Whether it's stress, anxiety, sadness, anger, or frustration, negative emotions can take a toll on our mental and physical health if not managed properly.

In this chapter, we'll explore the various types of negative thoughts and emotions, the impact they can have on our lives, and effective strategies for navigating them. We'll also discuss the importance of self-awareness, mindfulness, and positive habits in promoting inner peace and contentment.

Types of Negative Thoughts and Emotions

Negative thoughts and emotions can manifest in various forms, including:

Fear - Fear is a natural response to perceived danger or threat. However, when fear becomes excessive or irrational, it can lead to anxiety and panic attacks.

08: NAVIGATING NEGATIVE THOUGHTS AND EMOTIONS

Anger - Anger is a normal emotion that arises when we feel frustrated or powerless. However, unresolved anger can lead to aggression, hostility, and even violence.

Sadness - Sadness is a natural response to loss, disappointment, or grief. However, prolonged sadness can lead to depression and feelings of hopelessness.

Guilt - Guilt is a common emotion that arises when we believe we have done something wrong or hurtful. However, excessive guilt can lead to self-blame and low self-esteem.

Shame - Shame is a feeling of humiliation or disgrace that arises from a sense of inadequacy or failure. However, unresolved shame can lead to social withdrawal and isolation.

The Impact of Negative Thoughts and Emotions

Negative thoughts and emotions can have a significant impact on our mental and physical health. When left unchecked, they can lead to:

Chronic stress - Chronic stress can lead to a range of health problems, including high blood pressure, heart disease, and mental health issues such as anxiety and depression.

08: NAVIGATING NEGATIVE THOUGHTS AND EMOTIONS

Relationship problems - Negative thoughts and emotions can strain relationships with family, friends, and colleagues.

Poor performance - Negative thoughts and emotions can affect our ability to concentrate, remember, and perform well in school or work.

Substance abuse - Negative thoughts and emotions can lead to substance abuse as a way of coping with emotional pain.

Effective Strategies for Navigating Negative Thoughts and Emotions

Practice self-awareness - Self-awareness is the ability to recognize and understand our own emotions, thoughts, and behaviors. By developing self-awareness, we can identify our triggers and learn to respond to them in a healthy way.

Practice mindfulness - Mindfulness is the practice of being present in the moment and observing our thoughts and emotions without judgment. By practicing mindfulness, we can learn to detach from negative thoughts and emotions and view them from a more objective perspective.

Engage in positive habits - Positive habits, such as exercise, healthy eating, and good sleep hygiene, can improve our physical and mental health and help us manage negative thoughts and emotions more effectively.

Seek support - It's important to seek support from family, friends, or a mental health professional when dealing with negative thoughts and emotions. Talking about our problems with someone we trust can help us gain perspective and find solutions.

Conclusion

Navigating negative thoughts and emotions is an ongoing process that requires self-awareness, mindfulness, and positive habits. By developing these skills, we can learn to manage negative emotions more effectively and promote inner peace and contentment in our lives. Remember, it's okay to feel negative emotions, but it's how we respond to them that matters. With the right tools and support, we can transform our lives and find lasting serenity.

09: Overcoming Anxiety with Cognitive Behavioral Therapy

Anxiety is a common human experience, but for many people, it can become overwhelming and interfere with daily life. Anxiety disorders are the most common mental health disorders in the United States, affecting around 40 million adults. Fortunately, anxiety disorders are highly treatable, and cognitive-behavioral therapy (CBT) is one of the most effective treatments available.

CBT is a type of talk therapy that focuses on changing negative thoughts and behaviors that contribute to anxiety. The therapy is based on the idea that thoughts, feelings, and behaviors are interconnected, and that changing one can lead to changes in the others.

The first step in CBT is to identify the negative thoughts that are contributing to anxiety. These thoughts are often automatic and unconscious, but they can be brought to the surface through a process of introspection and reflection. Once the negative thoughts are identified, they can be challenged and replaced with more positive and realistic ones.

For example, a person with social anxiety might have the

automatic thought, "I always embarrass myself in social situations." This thought can be challenged by asking, "Is that really true? Have there been times when I didn't embarrass myself?" This can lead to the more positive thought, "I may have made mistakes in the past, but I am capable of having positive social interactions."

Another key component of CBT is exposure therapy. This involves gradually exposing the person to situations that trigger anxiety, in a safe and controlled way. Over time, the person learns to tolerate and even enjoy these situations, and the anxiety decreases.

For example, a person with a fear of flying might start by looking at pictures of airplanes, then watching videos of takeoffs and landings, then sitting in an airplane while it's on the ground, and eventually taking a short flight. By gradually exposing themselves to these situations, the person learns that they are not as dangerous as they thought, and the anxiety decreases.

In addition to cognitive restructuring and exposure therapy, CBT may also involve relaxation techniques such as deep breathing, progressive muscle relaxation, and visualization.

09: OVERCOMING ANXIETY WITH COGNITIVE BEHA-VIORAL THERAPY

These techniques can help reduce physical symptoms of anxiety, such as rapid heartbeat and sweating.

CBT is typically delivered in weekly or biweekly sessions with a trained therapist. The therapy is usually short-term, lasting between 8 and 20 sessions, although some people may benefit from longer-term therapy. CBT can be done individually or in a group setting.

In addition to working with a therapist, there are also many self-help resources available for CBT. These include books, online courses, and smartphone apps. These resources can be a helpful supplement to therapy or a standalone treatment for mild to moderate anxiety.

While CBT is highly effective for treating anxiety disorders, it is not a one-size-fits-all approach. Different people may respond better to different types of therapy, and it's important to find the right approach for each individual. Other therapies that may be effective for anxiety include mindfulness-based therapies, acceptance and commitment therapy, and psychodynamic therapy.

In addition to therapy, there are also many lifestyle changes that can help reduce anxiety. These include regular exercise, healthy eating, getting enough sleep, avoiding caffeine and alcohol, and practicing relaxation techniques. It's also important to identify and avoid triggers for anxiety, such as stressful situations or certain people.

In conclusion, cognitive-behavioral therapy is a highly effective treatment for anxiety disorders. By identifying and challenging negative thoughts, gradually exposing oneself to triggering situations, and practicing relaxation techniques, people can learn to manage and even overcome their anxiety. With the help of a trained therapist and self-help resources, anyone can learn to live a more peaceful and contented life.

10: Strategies for Coping with Stress and Burnout

Life can be incredibly demanding, and it's easy to become overwhelmed by the never-ending list of responsibilities, deadlines, and challenges. If you're constantly feeling stressed and burnt out, you're not alone. Many people struggle to maintain a healthy work-life balance and find inner peace amidst the chaos of modern life. Fortunately, there are numerous strategies and techniques that can help you cope with stress and burnout and achieve lasting serenity and fulfillment. In this chapter, we'll explore some of the most effective strategies for managing stress and avoiding burnout.

Mindfulness Meditation

Mindfulness meditation is a practice that involves paying attention to the present moment without judgment. By training your mind to focus on the present and let go of distracting thoughts, you can cultivate a sense of calm and inner peace that can help you cope with stress and anxiety. Regular mindfulness meditation practice has been shown to improve mood, increase feelings of well-being, and reduce symptoms of anxiety and depression.

10: STRATEGIES FOR COPING WITH STRESS AND BURNOUT

To practice mindfulness meditation, find a quiet place where you won't be disturbed. Sit comfortably with your back straight and your hands resting on your lap. Close your eyes and focus your attention on your breath. Notice the sensation of air flowing in and out of your nostrils or the rise and fall of your chest. Whenever your mind wanders, gently redirect your attention back to your breath. Continue this practice for 10-20 minutes each day, gradually increasing the amount of time as you become more comfortable with the practice.

Yoga

Yoga is a physical, mental, and spiritual practice that originated in ancient India. The practice involves a series of postures (asanas) and breathing exercises (pranayama) that can help improve flexibility, balance, strength, and overall physical health. In addition to the physical benefits, yoga can also help reduce stress and promote a sense of calm and relaxation.

There are many different styles of yoga, each with their own unique focus and approach. Some styles, like Hatha yoga, focus on slow, gentle movements and relaxation, while others, like Vinyasa yoga, involve more dynamic movements and a faster pace. Regardless of the style you choose, practicing yoga regularly can help you manage stress and improve your overall well-being.

Exercise

Regular exercise is one of the most effective ways to reduce stress and promote a sense of well-being. Exercise releases endorphins, which are natural mood-boosters that can help reduce feelings of stress and anxiety. Exercise also promotes better sleep, which is essential for overall physical and mental health.

There are many different types of exercise you can try, including cardio, strength training, and group fitness classes. The key is to find an activity that you enjoy and can realistically fit into your schedule. Aim for at least 30 minutes of moderate-intensity exercise most days of the week.

Gratitude Practice

Gratitude is a powerful practice that can help shift your focus from what you don't have to what you do have. By cultivating a sense of gratitude for the good things in your life, you can reduce feelings of stress and anxiety and promote a sense of well-being and contentment.

One way to practice gratitude is to keep a gratitude journal. Each day, write down three things you're grateful for. They can be big things, like a supportive family or a rewarding job, or small things, like a warm cup of tea or a sunny day. Taking time to acknowledge the good things in your life can help you stay focused on the positive and reduce feelings of stress and overwhelm.

Time Management

One of the biggest contributors to stress and burnout is a lack of time management. When we feel like we're constantly playing catch-up or have too much on our plate, it's easy to become overwhelmed and stressed. By learning how to manage your time effectively, you can reduce feelings of stress and create more space for the things that matter most to you.

One effective time management strategy is to prioritize your tasks. Make a list of everything you need to do and then rank them in order of importance. Focus on the most important tasks first, and then work your way down the list. This will help ensure that you're focusing your time and energy on the things that will have the greatest impact on your life and work.

Another effective time management strategy is to set boundaries. This means learning to say no to things that don't align with your priorities or that would cause you undue stress or overwhelm. It also means learning to delegate tasks when possible and recognizing when it's time to take a break or step back from a project or activity.

Self-Care

Self-care is an essential component of stress management and burnout prevention. Taking time to care for yourself can help you recharge your batteries, reduce feelings of stress and overwhelm, and promote a sense of well-being and contentment.

Self-care can take many different forms, depending on your preferences and needs. It might mean taking a relaxing bath, going for a walk in nature, spending time with loved ones, or indulging in a favorite hobby or activity. The key is to find activities that help you feel relaxed, happy, and rejuvenated.

Positive Thinking

Our thoughts and beliefs can have a powerful impact on our emotions and behavior. When we're constantly thinking negative thoughts or catastrophizing situations, it's easy to become overwhelmed and stressed. By practicing positive thinking, we can learn to reframe our thoughts in a more positive and empowering way, which can help reduce feelings of stress and promote a sense of well-being.

One effective way to practice positive thinking is to use affirmations. Affirmations are positive statements that we repeat to ourselves regularly to help reinforce positive beliefs and attitudes. Examples of affirmations might include "I am capable and competent," "I trust in my abilities," or "I am worthy of love and respect." By repeating these affirmations regularly, we can help retrain our brains to focus on the positive and reduce feelings of stress and negativity.

In conclusion, stress and burnout are common challenges in

today's fast-paced and demanding world. However, by practicing mindfulness, yoga, exercise, gratitude, time management, self-care, and positive thinking, we can learn to manage stress and find inner peace and contentment amidst the chaos of modern life. By taking care of ourselves and prioritizing our well-being, we can unlock our true potential and achieve lasting serenity and fulfillment.

11: The Connection between Sleep and Inner Peace

As we navigate our way through the ups and downs of modern life, it can be challenging to maintain a sense of peace and contentment. Stress, anxiety, and negative thoughts can all take their toll on our mental health and well-being. But did you know that one of the most powerful tools we have for achieving inner peace and tranquility is right within our reach every night? That's right: sleep.

In this chapter, we'll explore the fascinating connection between sleep and inner peace. We'll delve into the science behind why sleep is so important for our mental and emotional health, and we'll offer some practical tips and techniques for optimizing your sleep habits to achieve greater serenity and contentment in your waking life.

The Importance of Sleep for Inner Peace

First, let's take a closer look at why sleep is so crucial for achieving inner peace and contentment. When we sleep, our bodies and minds undergo a complex series of processes that are essential for our overall health and well-being. Here are just a few of the many benefits of a good night's sleep:

Improved mood: Lack of sleep is linked to an increased risk of depression and other mood disorders. When we get enough sleep, our brains are better equipped to regulate our emotions and manage stress, leading to greater overall happiness and contentment.

Reduced anxiety: Chronic sleep deprivation has been shown to increase anxiety levels, while getting enough sleep can help reduce feelings of worry and tension.

Enhanced cognitive function: Sleep is essential for optimal cognitive function, including memory consolidation, learning, and problem-solving. When we're well-rested, our brains are better able to process information, leading to greater clarity and focus.

Physical health benefits: Adequate sleep is also essential for maintaining our physical health. It helps to regulate our metabolism, support our immune system, and even promote healthy skin and hair.

The Science of Sleep

Now that we understand some of the many benefits of sleep

for our mental and emotional health, let's take a closer look at the science behind this essential process. Sleep is a complex process that involves several different stages, each with its unique characteristics and functions.

The first stage of sleep is known as NREM (non-rapid eye movement) sleep, which comprises about 75% of our total sleep time. During this stage, our brain waves slow down, and our bodies begin to relax. As we move into deeper stages of NREM sleep, our breathing and heart rate slow down, and our muscles become more relaxed.

The final stage of sleep is known as REM (rapid eye movement) sleep. This stage typically makes up around 25% of our total sleep time and is characterized by rapid eye movements and increased brain activity. During REM sleep, our bodies are effectively paralyzed, and our brain is highly active, processing emotions and memories and helping us to consolidate new information.

Optimizing Your Sleep Habits

Now that we understand the importance of sleep for achieving inner peace and contentment let's explore some practical tips and techniques for optimizing our sleep habits to get the most out of this essential process.

Establish a regular sleep schedule: One of the most important things you can do to optimize your sleep habits is to establish a regular sleep schedule. Try to go to bed and wake up at the same time every day, even on weekends.

Create a relaxing bedtime routine: Creating a relaxing bedtime routine can help signal to your body that it's time to wind down and prepare for sleep. This could include activities such as taking a warm bath, reading a book, or practicing meditation or deep breathing exercises.

Create a sleep-conducive environment: Make sure your sleeping environment is cool, quiet, and dark. Invest in a comfortable mattress and pillows, and consider using a white noise machine or earplugs to block out any external noise.

Limit screen time before bed: The blue light emitted by electronic devices can interfere with our body's natural sleep-wake cycle, making it harder to fall asleep. Try to limit your exposure to screens for at least an hour before bed.

Avoid caffeine and alcohol: Both caffeine and alcohol can disrupt our sleep patterns, making it harder to get a good night's rest. Try to avoid consuming these substances in the hours leading up to bedtime.

Get regular exercise: Regular exercise can help promote better sleep, as it helps to reduce stress and anxiety and promote relaxation. Just make sure to avoid exercising too close to bedtime, as this can actually make it harder to fall asleep.

Practice mindfulness: Practicing mindfulness can help quiet your mind and prepare you for a restful night's sleep. Try incorporating practices such as meditation, deep breathing, or progressive muscle relaxation into your bedtime routine.

By incorporating these habits and techniques into your daily routine, you can help optimize your sleep habits and achieve greater inner peace and contentment in your waking life.

Conclusion

As we've explored in this chapter, sleep is a powerful tool

11: THE CONNECTION BETWEEN SLEEP AND INNER PEACE

for achieving inner peace and contentment. By understanding the science behind this essential process and adopting healthy sleep habits and routines, we can harness the transformative power of sleep to improve our mental and emotional health, boost our cognitive function, and enhance our overall well-being. So tonight, as you prepare for bed, remember that a good night's sleep is not just a luxury but a necessity for achieving lasting serenity and fulfillment in the chaos of modern life.

12: The Benefits of a Healthy Diet for Serenity

The concept of serenity is often associated with a sense of inner peace and calmness, and it is often sought after in a world that is increasingly chaotic and stressful. While many factors contribute to our sense of wellbeing, there is a growing body of evidence that suggests that the food we eat can play a significant role in achieving and maintaining serenity.

In this chapter, we will explore the benefits of a healthy diet for serenity. We will discuss the impact that nutrition has on our mood, cognitive function, and overall wellbeing. We will also provide practical tips for incorporating healthy eating habits into your daily routine, so you can start reaping the benefits of a healthy diet for serenity today.

The Connection between Nutrition and Serenity

Before we dive into the specifics of how nutrition impacts serenity, it is essential to understand the connection between the two. Simply put, what we eat can directly affect our mood, emotions, and cognitive function. Studies have shown that a poor diet, high in sugar, saturated fats, and processed foods, can lead to an increased risk of depression, anxiety, and other mental health issues.

On the other hand, a healthy diet, rich in fruits, vegetables, whole grains, lean protein, and healthy fats, can help reduce stress, anxiety, and negative thoughts. This is because a healthy diet provides the body with the nutrients it needs to function correctly, which can positively impact our mental and emotional health.

The Benefits of a Healthy Diet for Serenity

Reduced Stress and Anxiety

One of the most significant benefits of a healthy diet for serenity is the reduction of stress and anxiety. When we eat a diet high in processed foods, sugar, and unhealthy fats, our bodies go into a state of inflammation, which can contribute to the development of anxiety and depression. On the other hand, a diet high in whole foods, such as fruits, vegetables, and whole grains, can help reduce inflammation and improve our mental and emotional health.

Improved Cognitive Function

Another benefit of a healthy diet for serenity is improved cognitive function. Our brains require a steady supply of nutrients to function correctly, and a diet high in fruits, vegetables, and healthy fats can provide those nutrients. Studies have shown that a diet rich in these foods can improve memory, focus, and concentration, which can help us feel more grounded and centered.

Increased Energy and Vitality

Eating a healthy diet can also increase our energy levels and overall vitality. When we eat a diet high in processed foods and unhealthy fats, we often feel sluggish and tired. However, when we eat a diet rich in whole foods, we provide our bodies with the nutrients they need to function optimally. This can result in increased energy levels, better sleep, and an overall sense of wellbeing.

Improved Digestion

A healthy diet can also improve our digestion, which can have a positive impact on our mental and emotional health. When we eat a diet high in processed foods, our digestive system can become sluggish and inefficient, which can lead to feelings of discomfort and irritability. On the other hand, when we eat a diet high in fiber, fruits, and vegetables, we support our digestive health, which can help us feel more calm and centered.

Tips for Incorporating Healthy Eating Habits into Your Daily Routine

Now that we have explored the benefits of a healthy diet for serenity, let's discuss some practical tips for incorporating healthy eating habits into your daily routine.

Start Your Day with a Healthy Breakfast

Starting your day with a healthy breakfast is one of the best things you can do for your mental and emotional health. A healthy breakfast should include a balance of protein, healthy fats, and complex carbohydrates. Some examples of healthy breakfast options include oatmeal with nuts and berries, a vegetable omelette with avocado, or a smoothie with spinach, fruit, and almond milk.

Focus on Whole Foods

One of the best ways to ensure that you are getting the nutrients your body needs is to focus on whole foods. This means choosing foods that are as close to their natural state as possible, such as fresh fruits and vegetables, whole grains, lean protein, and healthy fats. Avoid processed foods, which are often high in sugar, unhealthy fats, and additives that can contribute to inflammation and poor mental and emotional health.

Incorporate Mindful Eating Practices

Another way to support healthy eating habits is to incorporate mindful eating practices. This means paying attention to your food, savoring each bite, and eating slowly. When we eat mindfully, we are more likely to feel satisfied with smaller portions and less likely to overeat, which can help maintain a healthy weight and reduce feelings of stress and anxiety.

Drink Plenty of Water

Drinking plenty of water is essential for overall health and wellbeing, including mental and emotional health. Water helps flush toxins out of the body, regulates body temperature, and supports healthy digestion. Aim to drink at least eight glasses of water per day, and consider adding slices of lemon or cucumber for flavor.

12: THE BENEFITS OF A HEALTHY DIET FOR SERENITY

Plan Ahead

Finally, planning ahead can help ensure that you are making healthy food choices throughout the day. This might mean preparing meals and snacks ahead of time, or simply making a list of healthy foods to choose from when you are hungry. By having healthy options readily available, you can avoid the temptation of unhealthy snacks and fast food, which can negatively impact your mental and emotional health.

In conclusion, a healthy diet is essential for achieving and maintaining serenity. By choosing whole foods, incorporating mindful eating practices, and staying hydrated, you can support your mental and emotional health, reduce stress and anxiety, and unlock your true potential for lasting serenity and fulfillment. Remember, small changes can make a big difference, so start incorporating healthy eating habits into your daily routine today!

13: The Impact of Exercise on Mental Well-being

Exercise is one of the most powerful tools we have for promoting mental and physical health. It has been scientifically proven to reduce stress, anxiety, and depression, as well as improve cognitive function and overall well-being. In this chapter, we will explore the impact of exercise on mental well-being, the various types of exercise that can be beneficial, and how to incorporate exercise into your daily routine to achieve lasting serenity and inner peace.

The Benefits of Exercise on Mental Health

Exercise has numerous benefits for mental health. One of the most well-known benefits is its ability to reduce stress. When we exercise, our bodies release endorphins, which are natural mood-boosters that reduce stress and anxiety. This can help us feel more relaxed and calm, even in the midst of a hectic day.

Exercise also helps to improve cognitive function. When we exercise, blood flow to the brain increases, which can help improve memory, focus, and attention. In addition, regular exercise has been shown to promote the growth of new

brain cells, which can help to protect against cognitive decline.

Another benefit of exercise is its ability to promote better
sleep. Many people struggle with sleep issues, which can ex-
acerbate feelings of anxiety and depression. Exercise has
been shown to improve the quality of sleep, helping people
feel more rested and refreshed in the morning.

Exercise can also help to boost self-esteem and confidence.
When we engage in physical activity, we can feel a sense of
accomplishment and pride in our abilities. This can help to
improve our self-image and give us the confidence we need
to tackle other challenges in our lives.

Types of Exercise for Mental Well-being

There are many different types of exercise that can be beneficial for mental well-being. Some of the most popular forms
of exercise include:

Aerobic exercise - This includes activities such as running,
cycling, and swimming, which increase heart rate and oxygen consumption. Aerobic exercise has been shown to be

particularly effective for reducing symptoms of anxiety and depression.

Strength training - This involves lifting weights or using resistance bands to build muscle strength. Strength training has been shown to improve mood and cognitive function, as well as increase confidence and self-esteem.

Yoga - This is a form of exercise that combines physical postures, breathing exercises, and meditation. Yoga has been shown to reduce stress, anxiety, and depression, as well as improve overall well-being.

Mindful walking - This involves taking a leisurely walk while focusing on your surroundings and being present in the moment. Mindful walking has been shown to reduce stress and anxiety, as well as improve mood and cognitive function.

Tai chi - This is a gentle form of exercise that involves slow, flowing movements and deep breathing. Tai chi has been shown to reduce stress, anxiety, and depression, as well as improve balance and flexibility.

13: THE IMPACT OF EXERCISE ON MENTAL WELL-BE-ING

Incorporating Exercise into Your Daily Routine

In order to reap the benefits of exercise on mental well-being, it is important to make it a part of your daily routine. Here are some tips for incorporating exercise into your day:

Start small - If you are new to exercise, start with small, manageable goals. For example, aim to take a 10-minute walk each day and gradually increase the length of time as you become more comfortable.

Find an activity you enjoy - Exercise doesn't have to be a chore. Find an activity you enjoy, whether it's swimming, dancing, or hiking, and make it a part of your regular routine.

Make it social - Exercise can be a great way to connect with others. Consider joining a group fitness class or going for a walk with a friend.

Create a schedule - Treat exercise like any other appointment and schedule it into your day. This will help ensure that you make time for it and stick to your routine.

Mix it up - Variety is key when it comes to exercise. Try different activities to keep things interesting and prevent boredom.

Set goals - Setting goals can help you stay motivated and track your progress. Whether you want to run a 5K or lift a certain amount of weight, having a goal in mind can help keep you focused.

Make it a habit - Consistency is key when it comes to exercise. Make it a habit by doing it at the same time each day or week.

Listen to your body - It's important to listen to your body and not push yourself too hard. If you're feeling tired or sore, take a break and give yourself time to rest.

Get creative - Exercise doesn't have to be limited to traditional forms. Try dancing, gardening, or playing a sport to get moving and have fun.

Be patient - It takes time to see results from exercise. Don't get discouraged if you don't see immediate changes in your mental well-being. Stick with it and be patient.

Conclusion

13: THE IMPACT OF EXERCISE ON MENTAL WELL-BE-ING

Exercise is a powerful tool for promoting mental well-being. It can reduce stress, improve cognitive function, boost self-esteem, and promote better sleep. By incorporating exercise into your daily routine and trying different activities, you can achieve lasting serenity and inner peace. Remember to start small, find an activity you enjoy, and be patient as you work towards your goals. With time and consistency, exercise can transform your life and help you unlock your true potential.

14: Cultivating Gratitude and Appreciation

In a world where everything moves fast and people constantly chase after material wealth and success, it's easy to forget the importance of gratitude and appreciation. These two virtues are often overlooked but are actually the keys to unlocking inner peace and contentment. When you learn to cultivate gratitude and appreciation, you can experience the profound benefits of these virtues in your daily life.

Gratitude is the practice of being thankful for what you have, rather than focusing on what you lack. It's the act of acknowledging the good things in your life and expressing appreciation for them. When you cultivate gratitude, you shift your focus from what's missing to what's present, and this can have a powerful impact on your mental and emotional well-being.

Appreciation is similar to gratitude, but it's focused on recognizing the value of something or someone. When you appreciate something, you acknowledge its worth and express gratitude for its presence in your life. Appreciation can help you see the world in a more positive light, and it can foster deeper connections with the people and things around you.

14: CULTIVATING GRATITUDE AND APPRECIATION

So how can you cultivate gratitude and appreciation in your life? Here are some strategies that you can use to start practicing these virtues:

Keep a gratitude journal: One of the most effective ways to cultivate gratitude is to keep a daily gratitude journal. Each day, write down three things that you're thankful for, no matter how small or insignificant they may seem. This practice can help you develop a more positive mindset and increase your overall happiness.

Practice mindfulness: Mindfulness is the practice of being present in the moment and fully aware of your thoughts, feelings, and sensations. When you're mindful, you're more likely to notice the small things in life that bring you joy and appreciate them fully.

Express appreciation: Make a habit of expressing appreciation to the people in your life. Whether it's a simple thank-you note or a heartfelt conversation, expressing gratitude can deepen your relationships and help you feel more connected to others.

Find joy in the little things: Take time to notice the small things in life that bring you joy, such as a beautiful sunset or a hot cup of coffee. When you learn to appreciate these simple pleasures, you can cultivate a sense of gratitude for the abundance in your life.

Give back: Giving back to others is a powerful way to cultivate gratitude and appreciation. Whether it's volunteering at a local charity or simply helping a friend in need, acts of kindness can help you recognize the value of human connection and the positive impact you can have on others.

Practice self-care: Taking care of yourself is essential for cultivating gratitude and appreciation. When you prioritize your own well-being, you're more likely to appreciate the good things in your life and recognize the value of your own existence.

Surround yourself with positivity: Surrounding yourself with positive people and environments can help you cultivate gratitude and appreciation. Seek out friends and colleagues who inspire you, and spend time in places that uplift your spirits and bring you joy.

Incorporating these strategies into your daily life can help you cultivate a sense of gratitude and appreciation that can transform your outlook on life. When you learn to appreciate the small things and express gratitude for the abundance in your life, you can experience a profound sense of inner peace and contentment that can carry you through even the most challenging times.

15: Forgiveness and Letting Go of Resentment

Forgiveness and letting go of resentment are crucial components of achieving contentment and inner peace. Holding onto grudges and bitterness can create a negative cycle of thoughts and emotions, which can lead to increased stress, anxiety, and even physical health problems. In contrast, learning to forgive others and yourself can free you from the weight of negativity and allow you to move forward with positivity and clarity.

The act of forgiveness is often misunderstood. Many people believe that forgiving someone means condoning their actions or absolving them of responsibility. However, forgiveness is about releasing your own negative feelings towards someone and accepting that the past cannot be changed. It does not mean forgetting what happened or reconciling with the person who wronged you, but it does mean choosing to let go of the pain and anger associated with the situation.

Forgiveness is not always easy, especially when the hurt we have experienced is deep and long-lasting. However, it is a necessary step towards healing and finding peace. The following are some techniques that can help you on your journey towards forgiveness and letting go of resentment.

Acknowledge Your Feelings

The first step in forgiveness is to acknowledge your feelings. It is important to allow yourself to feel the pain, anger, and frustration associated with the situation. Trying to suppress or deny your emotions will only lead to increased stress and anxiety. Instead, take the time to sit with your feelings and allow yourself to fully experience them.

Practice Empathy

Empathy is the ability to understand and share the feelings of others. Practicing empathy towards the person who wronged you can help you to see things from their perspective and understand why they acted the way they did. This does not mean excusing their behavior, but it can help you to see them as human and flawed, rather than simply as a source of pain and anger.

Write a Letter

One powerful technique for letting go of resentment is to

write a letter to the person who wronged you. This letter is not meant to be sent, but rather is a way for you to express your feelings and work through your emotions. Write down everything that you want to say, including how the person's actions made you feel and the impact it had on your life. This can be a cathartic and healing process.

Practice Self-Compassion

Forgiving yourself is just as important as forgiving others. It is easy to be hard on ourselves and blame ourselves for past mistakes, but this only leads to increased stress and negative self-talk. Practicing self-compassion means treating yourself with the same kindness and understanding that you would offer to a friend. It means accepting your imperfections and mistakes and choosing to move forward with positivity and self-love.

Seek Support

Forgiveness is not always a solo journey. Seeking support from loved ones, a therapist, or a support group can provide you with the encouragement and guidance you need to move forward. Talking about your feelings and experiences can help you to gain perspective and find the strength to

15: FORGIVENESS AND LETTING GO OF RESENTMENT

forgive and let go of resentment.

In summary, forgiveness and letting go of resentment are essential components of achieving contentment and inner peace. These practices may not be easy, but they are necessary for your own mental and emotional wellbeing. By acknowledging your feelings, practicing empathy, writing a letter, practicing self-compassion, and seeking support, you can release the weight of negativity and find the peace and happiness you deserve.

16: The Importance of Self-Care in Achieving Serenity

In the chaos of modern life, it's easy to forget about the importance of taking care of oneself. We get caught up in our daily routines, our work, and our responsibilities, and often forget to prioritize our own physical, emotional, and mental well-being. However, self-care is essential for achieving lasting serenity and finding fulfillment in life.

Self-care refers to any intentional action taken to improve one's physical, emotional, or mental health. It includes activities such as exercise, meditation, journaling, and spending time with loved ones. Self-care is not a luxury; it's a necessity. It's important to take care of ourselves first before we can take care of others or tackle our responsibilities.

There are many benefits to practicing self-care. It can help reduce stress, improve overall well-being, and increase productivity. It can also lead to better relationships with others and a greater sense of fulfillment in life. Self-care is essential for achieving inner peace and lasting serenity.

One of the most important aspects of self-care is physical health. Taking care of one's physical health involves exercising regularly, eating a healthy diet, getting enough sleep, and taking care of any medical needs. Exercise has been shown to reduce stress and anxiety, improve mood, and boost self-confidence. Eating a healthy diet can also improve mood and energy levels, while getting enough sleep is essential for overall health and well-being.

Another important aspect of self-care is emotional health. Emotional self-care involves recognizing and addressing one's emotions, practicing mindfulness and relaxation techniques, and seeking support from loved ones or a mental health professional if needed. It's important to take time to process emotions and engage in activities that bring joy and fulfillment.

Mental health is also a crucial aspect of self-care. Mental self-care involves engaging in activities that promote mental well-being, such as meditation, journaling, or reading. It's important to prioritize mental health and seek help if necessary, such as speaking with a therapist or counselor.

Self-care can also involve setting boundaries and saying no to things that don't align with one's values or goals. It's important to prioritize what's truly important and not stretch oneself too thin. Saying no can be difficult, but it's essential for one's well-being.

It's also important to practice self-compassion and forgiveness. We all make mistakes, and it's important to treat ourselves with kindness and understanding. Forgiving ourselves for past mistakes and letting go of negative self-talk can help improve overall well-being and increase self-confidence.

Incorporating self-care into one's daily routine can be challenging, but it's essential for achieving lasting serenity and finding fulfillment in life. It's important to prioritize one's own well-being and take intentional actions to improve physical, emotional, and mental health. Practicing self-care can lead to a more balanced, fulfilling life and increased inner peace.

There are many ways to incorporate self-care into one's daily routine. Starting small and setting achievable goals can help build momentum and make self-care a regular habit. Some simple self-care practices include taking a relaxing bath, going for a walk in nature, listening to calming music, or reading a book. Other self-care practices may involve joining a fitness class, starting a new hobby, or taking a solo trip.

In conclusion, self-care is essential for achieving inner peace and lasting serenity. It's important to prioritize one's physical, emotional, and mental health and engage in intentional actions that promote well-being. Incorporating self-care into one's daily routine can lead to a more balanced, fulfilling life and increased inner peace. Remember, self-care is not a luxury; it's a necessity. Take care of yourself first, and the rest will fall into place.

17: Finding Purpose and Meaning in Life

Life is a journey that is often unpredictable, full of twists and turns that can lead us down paths we never thought we would take. It can be easy to lose our way and feel as though we are wandering aimlessly through the chaos of modern life. However, finding purpose and meaning in life is an essential component of achieving lasting contentment and serenity. In this chapter, we will explore the ways in which we can discover our purpose and find meaning in life.

The first step in finding purpose and meaning in life is to take the time to reflect on our values and beliefs. What is important to us? What motivates us? What brings us joy? By understanding our values and beliefs, we can begin to identify the things that give our lives purpose and meaning. This self-reflection can be done through journaling, meditation, or simply taking the time to sit quietly and think.

Once we have a better understanding of our values and beliefs, we can begin to set goals that align with our purpose and meaning. These goals can be short-term or long-term, but they should always be meaningful and aligned with our values. For example, if we value community service, we might set a goal to volunteer at a local shelter or food bank. If we value learning and growth, we might set a goal to enroll in a class or workshop that aligns with our interests.

It is important to remember that achieving our goals is not always easy, and setbacks and challenges are inevitable. However, it is through these challenges that we can learn and grow, ultimately leading us closer to our purpose and meaning. It is also important to be patient with ourselves and to practice self-compassion during the journey.

Another way to find purpose and meaning in life is to connect with others. Human connection is essential for our well-being and can provide us with a sense of belonging and purpose. We can connect with others through community service, joining clubs or organizations, or simply spending time with loved ones. It is important to surround ourselves with people who support and uplift us and who share our values and beliefs.

Finding purpose and meaning in life can also involve exploring our spirituality or beliefs. This can be done through religion, meditation, or other practices that allow us to connect with something greater than ourselves. Exploring our spirituality can help us find a deeper sense of purpose and meaning in life, as well as provide us with a sense of inner peace and serenity.

Another important component of finding purpose and meaning in life is to practice gratitude. Gratitude is the practice of focusing on the things we are thankful for and can help us cultivate a more positive outlook on life. By focusing on the things we are grateful for, we can shift our attention away from the things that bring us stress and anxiety and towards the things that bring us joy and fulfillment.

Finally, finding purpose and meaning in life involves living a life that is aligned with our values and beliefs. This means making choices that are in line with our purpose and meaning, and being true to ourselves. It can be easy to get caught up in the expectations of others or societal norms, but it is important to remember that our purpose and meaning in life are unique to us and cannot be defined by anyone else.

In conclusion, finding purpose and meaning in life is an ongoing journey that requires self-reflection, goal-setting, connecting with others, exploring spirituality, practicing gratitude, and living a life that is aligned with our values and beliefs. It is through this journey that we can discover the power of inner peace and transform our lives, finding lasting contentment and serenity in the chaos of modern life.

18: Pursuing Personal Growth and Development

Introduction

Personal growth and development are essential aspects of living a fulfilling life. It involves expanding our knowledge, developing new skills, and exploring our potential to achieve our goals and dreams. Pursuing personal growth and development is a continuous journey that involves self-reflection, self-improvement, and self-awareness.

In this chapter, we will explore the different aspects of personal growth and development and provide you with practical tips on how to achieve lasting serenity and find fulfillment in the chaos of modern life. From mindful practices to positive habits, you will learn how to overcome stress, anxiety, and negative thoughts and unlock your true potential with the ultimate self-help resource.

The Importance of Personal Growth and Development

Personal growth and development are important for several reasons. Firstly, it helps us to discover our true potential and talents. It allows us to explore new opportunities and experiences that we may not have considered before. Personal growth also helps us to become more self-aware and identify areas where we need to improve.

Secondly, personal growth and development can lead to increased confidence and self-esteem. As we develop new skills and knowledge, we become more confident in our abilities and feel better about ourselves. This, in turn, can lead to improved relationships, better job prospects, and a more positive outlook on life.

Thirdly, personal growth and development can help us to achieve our goals and dreams. By developing new skills and knowledge, we can overcome obstacles and challenges that may have previously held us back. It allows us to take control of our lives and create the future that we want.

As you can see, personal growth and development are essential aspects of living a fulfilling and satisfying life. It allows us to explore our potential, become more self-aware, and achieve our goals and dreams.

Identifying Your Personal Growth and Development Goals

18: PURSUING PERSONAL GROWTH AND DEVELOPMENT

Before you can start pursuing personal growth and development, you need to identify your goals. What is it that you want to achieve? What skills do you want to develop? What areas of your life do you want to improve?

To identify your personal growth and development goals, start by asking yourself some questions. Consider your current situation and what you want to achieve in the future. Some questions to consider include:

– What do I want to achieve in my career?

– What skills do I need to develop to achieve my career goals?

– What do I want to achieve in my personal life?

– What areas of my life do I want to improve?

– What new experiences do I want to have?

– What new skills do I want to develop?

Once you have identified your personal growth and development goals, you can start developing a plan to achieve them.

Developing a Plan for Personal Growth and Development

Developing a plan for personal growth and development involves setting goals and creating a plan to achieve them. Your plan should include specific actions that you can take to achieve your goals, such as:

– Learning new skills or knowledge

– Developing new habits or routines

– Seeking out new experiences

– Networking with others in your field

When creating your plan, it's important to be realistic about what you can achieve. Don't try to tackle too much at once, as this can be overwhelming and counterproductive. Instead, focus on one or two areas at a time and develop a plan to achieve your goals in those areas.

Tips for Personal Growth and Development

Here are some practical tips to help you achieve personal

growth and development:

Practice Mindfulness

Mindfulness is a powerful tool for personal growth and de-velopment. It involves being present in the moment and fully engaged in your surroundings. Mindfulness can help reduce stress, increase self-awareness, and improve your overall well-being. Consider incorporating mindfulness practices into your daily routine, such as meditation or deep breathing exercises.

Develop Positive Habits

Developing positive habits is essential for personal growth and development. Habits are behaviors that we do automat-ically, and they can have a significant impact on our lives. Positive habits can help us to become more productive, healthy, and happy. Consider identifying a few positive habits that you want to develop and start incorporating them into your daily routine.

Set Goals

Setting goals is an essential aspect of personal growth and

development. Goals give us something to work towards and can help us to stay motivated and focused. Make sure your goals are specific, measurable, and achievable. Write them down and track your progress regularly.

Seek out New Experiences

New experiences can help us to grow and develop as individuals. They allow us to step outside of our comfort zones and learn new things about ourselves and the world around us. Consider trying something new, whether it's a new hobby, traveling to a new place, or taking on a new challenge.

Read and Learn

Reading and learning are essential for personal growth and development. They allow us to expand our knowledge and develop new skills. Make a habit of reading books, articles, or blogs that relate to your personal growth goals. Take courses or attend workshops to develop new skills.

Seek Feedback

Feedback is a valuable tool for personal growth and development. It allows us to identify areas where we need to improve and make necessary changes. Seek feedback from others, whether it's from a mentor, colleague, or friend. Be open to constructive criticism and use it to improve yourself.

Practice Self-Care

Self-care is essential for personal growth and development. It involves taking care of your physical, emotional, and mental well-being. Make sure you are getting enough sleep, eating healthy, and exercising regularly. Practice activities that help you relax and de-stress, such as yoga or meditation.

Conclusion

Personal growth and development are essential for living a fulfilling life. It involves expanding our knowledge, developing new skills, and exploring our potential to achieve our goals and dreams. Pursuing personal growth and development is a continuous journey that involves self-reflection, self-improvement, and self-awareness.

18: PURSUING PERSONAL GROWTH AND DEVELOP-MENT

In this chapter, we explored the different aspects of personal growth and development and provided practical tips on how to achieve lasting serenity and find fulfillment in the chaos of modern life. From mindful practices to positive habits, you learned how to overcome stress, anxiety, and negative thoughts and unlock your true potential with the ultimate self-help resource.

Remember, personal growth and development is a journey, not a destination. It takes time, effort, and dedication to achieve your goals. Be patient with yourself, and enjoy the journey.

19: The Role of Relationships in Inner Peace

Relationships are an integral part of our lives, and they play a significant role in shaping our sense of self, our emotional well-being, and our overall happiness. Whether it is our relationship with family, friends, romantic partners, or colleagues, the people we interact with have a profound impact on our mental and emotional states. Thus, it is essential to understand the significance of relationships in achieving inner peace.

At its core, inner peace is the ability to remain calm and centered, even in the face of challenges and adversity. It is the state of mind that allows us to find serenity amidst the chaos of modern life. While inner peace is a personal journey, relationships can either help us in our quest for inner peace or hinder our progress.

Positive relationships are a source of support, encouragement, and love. They provide us with a sense of belonging, security, and connection. When we have healthy relationships, we feel validated and appreciated, which boosts our self-esteem and promotes a sense of inner peace.

19: THE ROLE OF RELATIONSHIPS IN INNER PEACE

On the other hand, toxic relationships can have a detrimental effect on our mental and emotional well-being. They can drain our energy, trigger stress and anxiety, and create feelings of insecurity and self-doubt. Toxic relationships are characterized by a lack of respect, trust, and empathy. They often involve emotional manipulation, criticism, and negative communication patterns.

One of the keys to achieving inner peace is to cultivate healthy relationships while distancing ourselves from toxic ones. To do so, we need to develop a sense of self-awareness and learn to recognize the signs of unhealthy relationships.

Self-awareness involves understanding our emotions, thoughts, and behaviors. When we are self-aware, we can recognize our triggers, identify our needs and values, and communicate them effectively to others. Self-awareness also helps us identify patterns in our relationships that may be contributing to our stress and anxiety.

For instance, if we are always seeking validation from others, we may attract people who are emotionally unavailable or who take advantage of our need for approval. By becoming self-aware of our need for validation, we can work on developing a stronger sense of self-worth and attracting healthier relationships.

Another key to cultivating healthy relationships is to practice empathy and active listening. Empathy involves putting ourselves in someone else's shoes and understanding their perspective. When we practice empathy, we can communicate more effectively, build trust, and deepen our connections with others.

Active listening involves giving our full attention to the person we are communicating with, without judgment or interruption. By actively listening, we can create a safe space for others to share their thoughts and feelings, which promotes a deeper sense of understanding and connection.

In addition to practicing empathy and active listening, it is essential to set boundaries in our relationships. Boundaries involve communicating our needs and values and expressing our limits. By setting boundaries, we can protect our emotional well-being and avoid toxic relationships.

For example, if we have a friend who is always negative and critical, we can set a boundary by communicating that we need positivity and support in our relationships. By setting this boundary, we can either encourage our friend to change their behavior or distance ourselves from the relationship if they are unwilling to respect our boundaries.

Lastly, it is important to cultivate a sense of gratitude and appreciation in our relationships. Gratitude involves acknowledging and appreciating the people in our lives who support and uplift us. When we practice gratitude, we shift our focus from what we lack to what we have, which promotes a sense of inner peace and contentment.

In conclusion, relationships play a significant role in achieving inner peace. Positive relationships can provide us with a sense of security, love, and connection, while toxic relationships can trigger stress, anxiety, and negative emotions. To cultivate healthy relationships, we need to practice self-awareness, empathy, active listening, setting boundaries, and gratitude. By doing so, we can create a supportive network of people who uplift us and contribute to our overall well-being.

One of the most important aspects of cultivating healthy relationships is to prioritize our own needs and values. It can be easy to fall into the trap of people-pleasing and sacrificing our own well-being for the sake of maintaining relationships. However, this can lead to feelings of resentment and burnout, which can hinder our progress towards inner peace.

Instead, it is essential to communicate our needs and boundaries clearly and assertively, even if it means risking conflict or discomfort in the short term. By prioritizing our own well-being, we can attract people who respect and support us, and cultivate relationships that contribute to our sense of inner peace.

Another important aspect of healthy relationships is to practice forgiveness and let go of grudges. Holding onto anger and resentment towards others can create a toxic cycle of negative emotions and behaviors that can hinder our progress towards inner peace.

Forgiveness involves acknowledging the harm that has been done and choosing to let go of the negative emotions associated with it. This does not mean that we condone harmful behavior or continue to engage in unhealthy relationships. Instead, it involves releasing the emotional attachment to the past and focusing on the present moment.

19: THE ROLE OF RELATIONSHIPS IN INNER PEACE

By practicing forgiveness, we can let go of the past and move forward with a sense of peace and contentment. This can lead to more fulfilling and positive relationships, as well as greater overall well-being.

Finally, it is essential to remember that achieving inner peace is a personal journey that requires consistent effort and practice. Cultivating healthy relationships is just one aspect of this journey, but it is an essential one that can significantly impact our mental and emotional well-being.

By prioritizing our own needs and values, practicing empathy and active listening, setting boundaries, cultivating gratitude, practicing forgiveness, and letting go of toxic relationships, we can create a supportive network of people that contribute to our sense of inner peace and overall well-being.

In conclusion, relationships are a crucial aspect of achieving inner peace. By cultivating healthy relationships and distancing ourselves from toxic ones, we can create a supportive network of people who uplift us and contribute to our overall well-being. Remember that achieving inner peace is a personal journey that requires consistent effort and practice, but with the right tools and mindset, we can find lasting serenity and fulfillment in the chaos of modern life.

20: Setting Boundaries and Learning to Say No

Introduction

In today's fast-paced world, it's easy to get caught up in the chaos and become overwhelmed. We often find ourselves saying yes to things we don't want to do, simply because we feel obligated or don't want to disappoint others. This can lead to feelings of resentment, stress, and anxiety, which can ultimately impact our mental and physical health.

In this chapter, we will explore the importance of setting boundaries and learning to say no. We'll discuss the benefits of establishing boundaries, the different types of boundaries, and provide you with practical tips to help you set and maintain your boundaries. We'll also discuss the challenges you may face when setting boundaries and offer solutions to help you overcome them.

Why Setting Boundaries is Important

Setting boundaries is crucial for our mental and emotional well-being. When we set boundaries, we are essentially defining what is and isn't acceptable in our relationships and interactions with others. Boundaries help us establish healthy relationships, promote self-respect and self-care, and prevent us from being taken advantage of or manipulated.

Without boundaries, we may find ourselves constantly saying yes to things we don't want to do, putting others' needs before our own, and sacrificing our own well-being for the sake of others. This can lead to feelings of resentment, burnout, and even depression.

Types of Boundaries

There are different types of boundaries we can set, including physical, emotional, and time boundaries.

Physical boundaries refer to our personal space and physical touch. These boundaries can be violated when someone invades our personal space or touches us inappropriately without our consent. It's important to establish physical boundaries to protect our safety and well-being.

Emotional boundaries refer to our feelings, thoughts, and beliefs. These boundaries can be violated when someone dismisses our emotions or invalidates our experiences.

Emotional boundaries are important because they allow us to express ourselves freely and feel heard and validated.

Time boundaries refer to our time and how we spend it. These boundaries can be violated when someone demands too much of our time or doesn't respect our schedule. Time boundaries are important because they allow us to prioritize our commitments and responsibilities and prevent us from becoming overwhelmed.

How to Set Boundaries

Setting boundaries can be challenging, especially if you're used to saying yes to everything. Here are some practical tips to help you set and maintain your boundaries:

Identify your boundaries: Before you can set boundaries, you need to know what they are. Take some time to reflect on what's important to you and what you're willing and not willing to tolerate in your relationships and interactions with others.

Communicate your boundaries: Once you've identified your boundaries, it's important to communicate them clearly and assertively. Be direct and specific about what you're comfortable with and what you're not comfortable with.

Be consistent: Setting boundaries is not a one-time thing. It's important to be consistent in enforcing your boundaries and not giving in to pressure or guilt.

Practice self-care: Setting boundaries can be challenging, so it's important to prioritize self-care. Take care of yourself physically, emotionally, and mentally, and make time for activities that bring you joy and fulfillment.

Challenges and Solutions

Setting boundaries can be challenging, and you may face resistance or pushback from others. Here are some common challenges you may face when setting boundaries and solutions to help you overcome them:

Feeling guilty: You may feel guilty for saying no or setting boundaries. It's important to remember that setting boundaries is not selfish, and you have the right to prioritize your well-being.

Fear of rejection: You may fear that setting boundaries will lead to rejection or conflict in your relationships. It's important to remember that healthy relationships are based on mutual respect and understanding, and that setting boundaries can actually strengthen your relationships by promoting honesty and trust.

Pressure from others: You may face pressure from others to say yes or compromise your boundaries. It's important to stay firm and remember that you have the right to set boundaries that align with your values and needs.

Lack of support: You may not receive support from others when setting boundaries. It's important to seek out a supportive community and surround yourself with people who respect and encourage your boundaries.

Conclusion

In conclusion, setting boundaries is essential for our mental and emotional well-being. It allows us to establish healthy relationships, promote self-respect and self-care, and prevent us from being taken advantage of or manipulated. Setting boundaries can be challenging, but with practice and consistency, it can become a natural and empowering habit. Remember to prioritize your well-being and communicate your boundaries assertively and consistently. By doing so, you'll unlock the power of inner peace and find fulfillment in the chaos of modern life.

21: Nurturing a Supportive Network

In today's fast-paced world, it is easy to feel overwhelmed and alone. We are constantly bombarded with news, social media, and work, leaving little time for self-reflection and connection with others. But research has shown that having a supportive network of family, friends, and community can greatly enhance our well-being and help us achieve contentment and serenity.

In this chapter, we will explore the importance of nurturing a supportive network and how you can build one that will sustain you through the ups and downs of life. From strengthening existing relationships to cultivating new ones, we will look at practical ways to connect with others and create a support system that empowers you.

Why a Supportive Network Matters

Humans are social beings, and we thrive on connection with others. We are wired to seek out relationships and form bonds with those around us. This is why loneliness and social isolation can have serious negative consequences on our mental and physical health.

21: NURTURING A SUPPORTIVE NETWORK

Studies have shown that individuals with strong social support systems are better able to cope with stress, have lower rates of depression and anxiety, and have a higher sense of well-being. They are also more likely to adopt healthy habits and behaviors, such as exercise, healthy eating, and getting enough sleep.

Having a supportive network also provides a sense of belonging and purpose. When we feel connected to others, we are more likely to feel valued and appreciated, and we have a greater sense of meaning and fulfillment in our lives.

Building a Supportive Network

Building a supportive network doesn't happen overnight. It takes time and effort to cultivate relationships and build trust with others. But the benefits are well worth it. Here are some practical ways to start building your support system today:

Strengthen existing relationships: Start by strengthening the relationships you already have. Reach out to friends and family members and make an effort to spend quality time with them. Schedule regular phone calls, coffee dates, or activities that you enjoy doing together.

Join groups or clubs: Look for groups or clubs that align with your interests or hobbies. This could be anything from a book club to a sports team to a volunteer organization. Joining a group or club can be a great way to meet like-minded people and build new relationships.

Attend events: Attend local events or community gatherings. This could be a farmers market, art festival, or fundraiser. Attend with an open mind and strike up conversations with others who are there. You never know who you might meet or what connections you might make.

Try online networking: Social media and online communities can be a great way to connect with others who share your interests or passions. Join Facebook groups or forums related to your hobbies or career. Engage in conversations and connect with others who share your values and beliefs.

Seek professional support: Sometimes, we need more than just friends and family to support us. Consider seeking professional support from a therapist, counselor, or coach. These individuals can provide a safe and supportive space for you to explore your feelings and work through challenges.

21: NURTURING A SUPPORTIVE NETWORK

Nurturing Relationships

Once you have started building your support system, it is important to nurture those relationships. Here are some tips for maintaining strong and healthy relationships:

Practice active listening: When you are with others, give them your full attention. Listen without judgment and try to understand their perspective. This can help build trust and deepen your connection with them.

Show gratitude: Express your gratitude and appreciation for those in your life. Let them know how much you value their friendship and support. This can help strengthen your bond and make them feel valued.

Be there for others: When someone in your support system needs help or support, be there for them. Offer a listening ear, a shoulder to cry on, or practical help if needed. This can help build trust and create a reciprocal relationship where both parties feel supported.

Practice forgiveness: No one is perfect, and conflicts are bound to arise in any relationship. It is important to practice forgiveness and let go of grudges or resentments. This can help strengthen your relationships and create a more positive and supportive environment.

Set boundaries: While it is important to be there for others, it is also important to set boundaries and take care of yourself. Be clear about your needs and limitations, and communicate them with others. This can help prevent burnout and ensure that your relationships are healthy and sustainable.

Conclusion

Building and nurturing a supportive network is essential for achieving contentment and serenity in our lives. By connecting with others and building relationships based on trust, respect, and mutual support, we can create a strong foundation for our well-being and happiness.

Remember that building a supportive network takes time and effort, but the benefits are well worth it. Whether it is strengthening existing relationships, joining groups or clubs, attending events, trying online networking, or seeking professional support, there are many practical ways to start building your support system today.

And once you have started building those relationships, remember to nurture them through active listening, gratitude, forgiveness, being there for others, and setting boundaries. By doing so, you can create a network of support that will sustain you through the ups and downs of life and help you achieve lasting serenity and fulfillment.

22: Building Resilience and Coping Skills

Life can be challenging at times, and we all face obstacles, setbacks, and hardships that can test our resilience and coping skills. Whether it's a major life change like a job loss or a breakup, or ongoing stressors like financial pressures or health issues, learning how to build resilience and cope effectively is essential to maintaining our mental and emotional well-being.

In this chapter, we will explore what resilience and coping skills are, why they are important, and how to cultivate them in your own life. We'll also discuss some common obstacles to resilience and coping, and offer practical strategies for overcoming them.

What is Resilience?

Resilience is the ability to adapt to adversity, overcome challenges, and bounce back from setbacks. It's a trait that enables us to cope with stress and hardship without losing our sense of self or giving up on our goals and aspirations. Resilient individuals are not immune to life's challenges, but they are better equipped to manage them and recover from them.

Why is Resilience Important?

Resilience is important for several reasons. First, it helps us cope with stress and adversity, which is essential for maintaining our mental and emotional well-being. Second, it enables us to pursue our goals and aspirations despite obstacles and setbacks, which is essential for personal growth and development. Finally, resilience helps us build stronger relationships and connections with others, as it allows us to be more empathetic, compassionate, and supportive in our interactions.

What are Coping Skills?

Coping skills are the strategies and techniques we use to manage stress, regulate our emotions, and navigate challenging situations. Effective coping skills can help us reduce anxiety, improve mood, and increase our sense of control and self-efficacy.

Why are Coping Skills Important?

Coping skills are important for several reasons. First, they help us manage stress and anxiety, which is essential for maintaining our mental and emotional well-being. Second, they help us build resilience and bounce back from setbacks, which is essential for pursuing our goals and aspirations. Finally, coping skills can improve our relationships and social support networks, as they allow us to communicate more effectively and handle conflict in a healthy and constructive way.

Building Resilience and Coping Skills

So how can you build resilience and coping skills in your own life? Here are some strategies to get you started:

Practice Self-Care: Taking care of yourself is essential for building resilience and coping skills. Make sure you are getting enough sleep, eating a healthy diet, exercising regularly, and engaging in activities that bring you joy and fulfillment.

Practice Mindfulness: Mindfulness is the practice of being present in the moment, without judgment. It can help you regulate your emotions, reduce stress, and improve your overall well-being. Try incorporating mindfulness practices like meditation, deep breathing, or yoga into your daily routine.

Develop a Growth Mindset: A growth mindset is the belief that you can learn and grow from your experiences, even when they are challenging. Cultivating a growth mindset can help you see setbacks and failures as opportunities for learning and growth, rather than sources of discouragement.

Build Strong Relationships: Building strong relationships with family, friends, and colleagues can provide a valuable source of support and encouragement when facing adversity. Make an effort to connect with others, express gratitude and appreciation, and seek out opportunities for social connection.

Seek Professional Help: If you are struggling with mental health issues like anxiety or depression, seek professional help. A mental health professional can provide you with the tools and support you need to build resilience and cope effectively with life's challenges.

Obstacles to Resilience and Coping

While building resilience and coping skills is essential for maintaining our mental and emotional well-being, it's important to recognize that there are common obstacles that can get in the way. Here are some common obstacles to resilience and coping, and strategies for overcoming them:

Negative Self-Talk: Negative self-talk can be a major obstacle to resilience and coping. It can undermine our confidence and self-efficacy, and make us feel helpless and overwhelmed. To overcome negative self-talk, try practicing self-compassion and reframing your thoughts in a more positive and constructive way.

Perfectionism: Perfectionism is the belief that we must be perfect in order to be worthy and successful. It can lead to unrealistic expectations, self-criticism, and a fear of failure. To overcome perfectionism, try setting realistic goals, practicing self-compassion, and focusing on progress rather than perfection.

Lack of Social Support: A lack of social support can make it difficult to build resilience and cope with stress. To overcome this obstacle, try reaching out to others, joining a support group, or seeking professional help.

Avoidance: Avoidance is the tendency to avoid or ignore

stressors rather than confronting them. While avoidance may provide temporary relief, it can make the underlying problem worse in the long run. To overcome avoidance, try facing your fears and challenges head-on, and developing a plan for managing them.

Negative Coping Strategies: Negative coping strategies like substance abuse, overeating, or self-harm can provide temporary relief from stress, but can ultimately lead to more problems. To overcome negative coping strategies, try replacing them with more positive and constructive coping strategies like exercise, mindfulness, or creative expression.

Conclusion

Building resilience and coping skills is essential for maintaining our mental and emotional well-being in the face of life's challenges. By practicing self-care, mindfulness, and developing a growth mindset, we can learn to bounce back from setbacks, pursue our goals and aspirations, and build stronger relationships with others. While there may be obstacles to resilience and coping, with the right strategies and support, we can overcome them and unlock our true potential for happiness and fulfillment.

23: Cultivating a Positive Mindset

The power of the mind is truly incredible. It has the ability to create our reality, shape our experiences, and influence our emotions. Our thoughts, beliefs, and attitudes are the driving forces behind our actions and behaviors, which ultimately determine our level of happiness and contentment in life. Therefore, cultivating a positive mindset is crucial for achieving lasting serenity and finding fulfillment in the chaos of modern life.

Positive thinking is not just a fleeting emotion or temporary mood. It is a way of life that involves shifting our perspective and outlook towards the world. It involves recognizing the good in every situation, focusing on our strengths and abilities, and having faith in ourselves and our future. A positive mindset is not about ignoring the negative aspects of life, but rather, choosing to approach them in a constructive and productive manner.

The first step in cultivating a positive mindset is to become aware of our thoughts and emotions. We need to observe and acknowledge our negative self-talk and beliefs, and challenge them with positive affirmations and self-talk. This requires mindfulness and self-awareness, which can be achieved through meditation, journaling, or simply taking a few minutes each day to reflect on our thoughts and feelings.

Another important aspect of cultivating a positive mindset is to practice gratitude. Gratitude is the act of expressing appreciation for the good things in our lives, no matter how small they may be. It involves focusing on what we have rather than what we lack, and recognizing the abundance and blessings that surround us. By practicing gratitude regularly, we train our minds to see the positive aspects of life and appreciate the present moment.

In addition to practicing gratitude, it is also important to surround ourselves with positivity. This can involve spending time with positive and uplifting people, reading inspirational books and quotes, or listening to motivational podcasts or speeches. We become the company we keep, and by surrounding ourselves with positivity, we create a supportive and encouraging environment that nourishes our positive mindset.

Another effective way to cultivate a positive mindset is to set goals and visualize success. By setting achievable goals and visualizing ourselves achieving them, we create a sense of purpose and direction in our lives. This helps us to stay motivated and focused, and gives us a sense of accomplishment and satisfaction when we reach our goals. Visualization is a powerful tool that can help us manifest our desires and dreams into reality, and can help us overcome obstacles and challenges along the way.

Finally, it is important to practice self-care and self-compassion. We need to treat ourselves with kindness, understanding, and forgiveness, and recognize that we are all human and make mistakes. By practicing self-care, we nourish our physical, emotional, and spiritual well-being, and by practicing self-compassion, we cultivate a positive and loving relationship with ourselves. This helps us to develop a strong sense of self-worth and confidence, which in turn, supports our positive mindset.

In conclusion, cultivating a positive mindset is essential for achieving lasting serenity and finding fulfillment in the chaos of modern life. By becoming aware of our thoughts and emotions, practicing gratitude, surrounding ourselves with positivity, setting goals and visualizing success, and practicing self-care and self-compassion, we can train our minds to see the good in every situation and create a life filled with peace, happiness, and contentment. It takes time, effort, and commitment, but the rewards are immeasurable.

24: Embracing Change and Uncertainty

Life is unpredictable. It is full of twists and turns, and no matter how much we try to control it, we can never predict what will happen next. Change is the only constant in life, and uncertainty is a part of the journey. While some people thrive in the face of uncertainty, others find it overwhelming and paralyzing. However, the key to living a fulfilling life is to learn how to embrace change and uncertainty.

Embracing change and uncertainty requires a shift in mindset. It requires us to let go of our need for control and certainty and to trust that everything will work out in the end. This is not always easy, especially if we have experienced trauma or significant life changes that have left us feeling vulnerable and insecure. However, with the right mindset and tools, we can learn to embrace change and uncertainty and find peace amidst the chaos.

The first step in embracing change and uncertainty is to acknowledge that we cannot control everything. We must accept that life is unpredictable and that unexpected events will happen. This can be difficult, especially for those who have a strong need for control. However, by acknowledging this fact, we can begin to let go of our need for certainty and start to focus on what we can control.

The next step is to cultivate a growth mindset. This means embracing challenges and seeing them as opportunities for growth and learning. When we approach challenges with a growth mindset, we are more likely to be resilient and to bounce back from setbacks. We can also learn to see change as an opportunity for growth and to embrace it as a natural part of the journey.

Another key to embracing change and uncertainty is to practice mindfulness. Mindfulness is the practice of being present and fully engaged in the current moment. It can help us to let go of our worries about the future and to focus on the present moment. When we are mindful, we can observe our thoughts and emotions without judgment, and we can learn to respond to situations with calmness and clarity.

Another helpful tool for embracing change and uncertainty is to develop a sense of purpose. When we have a sense of purpose, we are more likely to be resilient and to stay focused on our goals, even when things get tough. We can also use our sense of purpose as a guidepost to help us navigate the uncertain waters of life.

Finally, it is important to build a strong support system. This can include friends, family, or a therapist or coach. When we have a strong support system, we are more likely to be resilient and to cope with the challenges of life. We can also use our support system to help us stay focused on our goals and to remind us of our strengths and capabilities.

In conclusion, embracing change and uncertainty is a key component of living a fulfilling life. While it can be challenging, with the right mindset and tools, we can learn to embrace change and uncertainty and find peace amidst the chaos. By acknowledging that we cannot control everything, cultivating a growth mindset, practicing mindfulness, developing a sense of purpose, and building a strong support system, we can learn to thrive in the face of uncertainty and to live a life of contentment and serenity.

25: Letting Go of Perfectionism and Embracing Imperfection

As human beings, we often strive for perfection. We want to be the best versions of ourselves, excel in our careers, have perfect relationships, and live a life free of stress and anxiety. However, the reality is far from perfect. We make mistakes, we face challenges, we have moments of weakness, and we often fall short of our expectations. In this chapter, we will discuss the importance of letting go of perfectionism and embracing imperfection in order to achieve contentment and serenity in our lives.

Perfectionism is a mindset that is characterized by a relentless pursuit of flawlessness and an inability to accept anything less than perfect. It is often associated with high standards, a strong work ethic, and a desire for excellence. While these may seem like positive attributes, perfectionism can actually have a negative impact on our lives. It can lead to feelings of anxiety, stress, and self-doubt, as well as a constant sense of dissatisfaction with our achievements.

The root of perfectionism often lies in our childhood experiences. We may have grown up in an environment where perfection was expected or praised, or we may have experienced a traumatic event that made us feel like we needed to be perfect in order to be loved or accepted. Whatever the cause, it is important to recognize the negative impact that perfectionism can have on our lives and take steps to overcome it.

One of the first steps in overcoming perfectionism is to recognize that perfection is unattainable. No matter how hard we try, we will never be perfect. There will always be something that we could have done better or something that we could have improved upon. Accepting this reality can be difficult, but it is an important step in letting go of perfectionism.

Another step in overcoming perfectionism is to practice self-compassion. Instead of criticizing ourselves for our mistakes and shortcomings, we need to learn to be kind and understanding to ourselves. We need to recognize that we are human, and that making mistakes is a natural part of the learning process. By treating ourselves with compassion and understanding, we can begin to let go of our perfectionistic tendencies and embrace imperfection.

Mindfulness practices can also be helpful in overcoming

perfectionism. Mindfulness involves being present in the moment and accepting things as they are, without judgment or criticism. By practicing mindfulness, we can learn to let go of our perfectionistic tendencies and focus on the present moment. We can learn to appreciate the beauty in imperfection and recognize that imperfection is what makes us human.

Another way to embrace imperfection is to develop a growth mindset. A growth mindset is characterized by a belief that we can learn and grow from our mistakes and failures. Instead of seeing our mistakes as evidence of our inadequacy, we can view them as opportunities for growth and learning. By adopting a growth mindset, we can let go of our perfectionistic tendencies and focus on our personal growth and development.

In addition to these strategies, it is important to develop positive habits that support our mental and emotional well-being. This may include engaging in regular exercise, eating a healthy diet, getting enough sleep, and practicing self-care. By taking care of ourselves in these ways, we can build resilience and develop the strength to overcome our perfectionistic tendencies.

Ultimately, letting go of perfectionism and embracing imperfection is a journey that requires patience, self-compassion, and a willingness to change. By recognizing the negative impact that perfectionism can have on our lives and taking steps to overcome it, we can achieve contentment and serenity in our lives. We can learn to appreciate the beauty in imperfection and recognize that imperfection is what makes us human. So, let go of perfectionism and embrace imperfection – it may just be the key to unlocking your true potential and finding lasting fulfillment in the chaos of modern life.

It's important to note that letting go of perfectionism doesn't mean that we lower our standards or stop striving for excellence. Rather, it means that we learn to approach our goals with a healthy and balanced mindset. We learn to set realistic expectations for ourselves and recognize that making mistakes and facing setbacks is a natural part of the process. We learn to celebrate our successes, no matter how small, and use our failures as opportunities for growth and learning.

25: LETTING GO OF PERFECTIONISM AND EMBRACING IMPERFECTION

One of the challenges of letting go of perfectionism is that it can be deeply ingrained in our identity and self-worth. We may have spent years striving for perfection, and the thought of letting go of this mindset can be intimidating. However, by taking small steps towards letting go of perfectionism, we can begin to shift our mindset and develop a healthier relationship with ourselves.

One way to do this is to focus on progress rather than perfection. Instead of striving for perfection, we can focus on making progress towards our goals. We can celebrate our small wins and recognize that each step we take towards our goals is a step in the right direction. By shifting our focus from perfection to progress, we can develop a more balanced and sustainable approach to achieving our goals.

Another way to let go of perfectionism is to practice self-acceptance. This means accepting ourselves for who we are, flaws and all. We can learn to recognize our strengths and weaknesses and appreciate the unique qualities that make us who we are. By practicing self-acceptance, we can begin to let go of our need for perfection and develop a more positive and realistic view of ourselves.

25: LETTING GO OF PERFECTIONISM AND EMBRACING IMPERFECTION

Finally, it's important to seek support and guidance from others. Letting go of perfectionism can be a challenging and emotional process, and it can be helpful to have the support of friends, family, or a professional counselor. They can offer guidance, feedback, and encouragement as we work towards letting go of our perfectionistic tendencies and embracing imperfection.

In conclusion, letting go of perfectionism and embracing imperfection is a powerful way to achieve contentment and serenity in our lives. By recognizing the negative impact that perfectionism can have on our mental and emotional well-being and taking steps to overcome it, we can develop a healthier and more balanced approach to achieving our goals. We can learn to appreciate the beauty in imperfection, celebrate our successes, and use our failures as opportunities for growth and learning. With patience, self-compassion, and a willingness to change, we can unlock our true potential and find lasting fulfillment in the chaos of modern life.

26: Tapping into Your Inner Strength and Courage

Introduction:

Life can be a rollercoaster ride, with ups and downs, twists and turns, and unexpected surprises at every turn. It's easy to get lost in the chaos of modern life and lose sight of what's truly important. However, it's during these challenging times that we need to tap into our inner strength and courage to push through and come out stronger on the other side.

In this chapter, we'll explore the importance of cultivating inner strength and courage, and how you can tap into these qualities to overcome challenges and live a more fulfilling life. We'll also look at some practical tips and techniques for developing these qualities, so you can start unlocking your true potential today.

What is Inner Strength and Courage?

Inner strength and courage are two qualities that are essential for achieving lasting serenity and finding fulfillment in life. Inner strength is the ability to remain resilient in the face of adversity, while courage is the willingness to take action despite fear or uncertainty.

These qualities are closely intertwined, as inner strength enables us to push through difficult times and find the courage to take risks and pursue our goals. They are also qualities that can be developed and strengthened through practice and dedication.

Why is Inner Strength and Courage Important?

Developing inner strength and courage is important for a number of reasons. Firstly, it enables us to overcome challenges and obstacles that we may encounter in life. Whether it's a personal setback or a global crisis, having the resilience and courage to push through and keep moving forward is essential for success.

Secondly, inner strength and courage are essential for personal growth and development. When we have the courage to step outside of our comfort zone and take risks, we open ourselves up to new opportunities and experiences that can help us grow and develop as individuals.

Finally, cultivating inner strength and courage can also have a positive impact on our mental and physical health. Research has shown that people who possess these qualities are more likely to experience lower levels of stress and anxiety, and are more resilient in the face of adversity.

How to Cultivate Inner Strength and Courage

Practice Self-Awareness:

The first step to cultivating inner strength and courage is to develop self-awareness. This means taking the time to reflect on your thoughts, emotions, and behaviors, and gaining a deeper understanding of yourself.

When we are self-aware, we are better able to recognize our strengths and weaknesses, and develop strategies for overcoming challenges and pushing through difficult times.

Set Goals and Take Action:

Setting goals and taking action is another key component of cultivating inner strength and courage. When we set goals, we give ourselves something to strive for, and when we take action towards those goals, we build momentum and momentum builds motivation.

It's important to set realistic goals that are challenging but achievable, and to break them down into smaller steps that are easier to tackle. This will help you stay motivated and build momentum over time.

Develop Positive Habits:

Developing positive habits is another important step in cultivating inner strength and courage. When we develop positive habits, we create a structure and routine that supports our goals and helps us stay focused and motivated.

Some examples of positive habits include practicing meditation or mindfulness, exercising regularly, eating a healthy diet, getting enough sleep, and spending time with loved ones.

Cultivate Resilience:

Resilience is a key component of inner strength, and it's something that can be developed through practice. Resilience is the ability to bounce back from setbacks and difficulties, and to remain optimistic and positive in the face of adversity.

One way to cultivate resilience is to practice reframing negative situations in a more positive light. This involves looking for the silver lining in difficult situations and focusing on the lessons learned rather than dwelling on the negative aspects.

Embrace Change:

Embracing change is another important aspect of cultivating inner strength and courage. Change can be scary, but it's also an opportunity for growth and development. When we embrace change, we open ourselves up to new experiences and opportunities, and we become more adaptable and resilient in the face of uncertainty.

To embrace change, it's important to be open-minded and flexible. Instead of resisting change, try to approach it with curiosity and a willingness to learn. Look for the positives in the situation and focus on the opportunities it presents.

Practice Self-Compassion:

Finally, practicing self-compassion is an important part of

cultivating inner strength and courage. Self-compassion involves treating ourselves with kindness and understanding,
and being gentle with ourselves when we make mistakes or
face setbacks.

When we practice self-compassion, we are better able to
bounce back from setbacks and challenges, and we become
more resilient and confident in the face of adversity. Some
ways to practice self-compassion include practicing self-
care, being kind to ourselves in our self-talk, and treating
ourselves as we would treat a good friend.

Conclusion:

Developing inner strength and courage is essential for
achieving lasting serenity and finding fulfillment in life.
These qualities enable us to overcome challenges, take risks,
and pursue our goals with confidence and resilience. By
practicing self-awareness, setting goals, developing positive
habits, cultivating resilience, embracing change, and practicing self-compassion, we can tap into our inner strength
and courage and unlock our true potential.

27: Overcoming Fears and Limiting Beliefs

Introduction

Do you ever feel like something is holding you back from achieving your dreams and living the life you truly want? Maybe it's fear of failure, fear of rejection, or limiting beliefs that you've internalized over the years. Whatever it is, it's time to overcome these obstacles and unlock your true potential. In this chapter, we will explore the ways in which you can overcome your fears and limiting beliefs to achieve inner peace and contentment.

Understanding Fears and Limiting Beliefs

Fears and limiting beliefs are often rooted in our past experiences and beliefs about ourselves and the world around us. For example, if you were criticized for your writing in school, you may have developed a fear of writing or a limiting belief that you're not a good writer. These fears and beliefs can hold us back in various areas of our lives, from our careers to our relationships.

The first step to overcoming your fears and limiting beliefs is to identify them. Take some time to reflect on your thoughts and emotions in different situations. What are you afraid of? What limiting beliefs do you hold about yourself or the world around you? Once you've identified your fears and limiting beliefs, you can start working on overcoming them.

Overcoming Fears

One of the most common fears that people experience is the fear of failure. This fear can hold you back from pursuing your goals and dreams, as you may be afraid of the potential consequences of not succeeding. To overcome this fear, it's important to shift your mindset from failure being a negative outcome to a learning experience. Every failure is an opportunity to learn and grow, and it's often the setbacks that lead to the most significant breakthroughs.

Another common fear is the fear of rejection. This fear can be paralyzing, as it can prevent you from taking risks and putting yourself out there. To overcome this fear, it's important to remember that rejection is not a reflection of your worth as a person. People reject ideas and proposals, not individuals. Reframe rejection as an opportunity to learn and improve your approach, and keep pushing forward.

Overcoming Limiting Beliefs

Limiting beliefs are often deeply ingrained in our subconscious, and it can take time and effort to overcome them. One common limiting belief is the belief that we're not good enough. This belief can manifest in different ways, from imposter syndrome in the workplace to feelings of inadequacy in relationships. To overcome this limiting belief, it's important to focus on your strengths and accomplishments. Make a list of your achievements, no matter how small, and celebrate them. Challenge the negative self-talk that reinforces the belief that you're not good enough and replace it with positive affirmations.

Another limiting belief that can hold you back is the belief that you're stuck in your current situation. This belief can prevent you from taking action and making changes in your life. To overcome this belief, it's important to focus on the power of choice. You always have the power to choose your actions and reactions, even in challenging situations. Take small steps towards your goals, and focus on progress rather than perfection.

Practical Strategies for Overcoming Fears and Limiting Beliefs

In addition to the mindset shifts mentioned above, there are several practical strategies you can use to overcome your fears and limiting beliefs.

Practice Mindfulness

Mindfulness is the practice of being present in the moment, without judgment or distraction. By practicing mindfulness, you can become more aware of your thoughts and emotions, and learn to respond to them in a more constructive way. This can help you to overcome fears and limiting beliefs by reducing the power they have over you.

Use Positive Visualization

Visualizing success and positive outcomes can be a powerful tool for overcoming fears and limiting beliefs. Take some time to visualize yourself achieving your goals in detail, imagining every step along the way and how it will feel when you accomplish them. This can help to shift your mindset from one of doubt and fear to one of confidence and optimism.

Challenge Your Beliefs

It's important to challenge your limiting beliefs by questioning their validity. Ask yourself why you believe something to be true and whether there is evidence to support it. Often, our limiting beliefs are based on assumptions or past experiences that may no longer be relevant. By challenging your beliefs, you can begin to see things in a new light and overcome the limitations they place on you.

Take Action

Taking action is one of the most powerful ways to overcome fears and limiting beliefs. When you take action, you prove to yourself that you are capable of achieving your goals and that your fears and limiting beliefs are unfounded. Start small by taking a small step towards your goal and build momentum from there.

Conclusion

Overcoming fears and limiting beliefs is essential if you

want to achieve lasting serenity and find fulfillment in the chaos of modern life. By identifying your fears and limiting beliefs, shifting your mindset, and using practical strategies to overcome them, you can unlock your true potential and live the life you've always dreamed of. Remember, you have the power to choose your thoughts and actions, and by choosing to overcome your fears and limiting beliefs, you can achieve inner peace and contentment.

28: Discovering Your Values and Priorities

In today's fast-paced world, it's easy to get lost in the chaos of modern life. We're bombarded with information from every direction, and it's easy to lose sight of what's truly important. That's why it's essential to take the time to discover your values and priorities.

Understanding your values and priorities is key to living a fulfilling life. It helps you make decisions that are aligned with your goals and what matters most to you. It also helps you focus on the things that bring you joy and satisfaction, while letting go of the things that don't.

So how do you discover your values and priorities? It starts by taking a step back and looking inward. Ask yourself, "What's most important to me?" "What do I value?" "What do I want to achieve in life?" "What kind of person do I want to be?"

Reflecting on these questions can help you identify your core values and priorities. These might include things like family, health, spirituality, career, education, community service, creativity, adventure, or personal growth.

28: DISCOVERING YOUR VALUES AND PRIORITIES

Once you've identified your values and priorities, the next step is to make them a priority in your life. This means setting goals and taking action to achieve them. For example, if you value your health, you might set a goal to exercise for 30 minutes each day. If you value your family, you might prioritize spending quality time with them each week.

It's also important to align your values and priorities with your daily habits and routines. This means making conscious choices about how you spend your time and energy. For example, if you value creativity, you might prioritize time each day for writing, painting, or playing music. If you value community service, you might volunteer at a local charity or organization.

It's important to remember that discovering your values and priorities is an ongoing process. As you grow and evolve, your values may shift and change. That's okay. What's important is to stay true to yourself and continue to prioritize the things that matter most to you.

In addition to reflecting on your values and priorities, there are other strategies you can use to cultivate inner peace and contentment. Mindful practices like meditation, yoga, and deep breathing can help you stay centered and calm in the face of stress and anxiety. Positive self-talk and affirmations can help you overcome negative thoughts and build self-confidence. Journaling and gratitude practices can help you cultivate a sense of appreciation and joy in your life.

Ultimately, discovering your values and priorities is about taking control of your life and living with intention. It's about creating a life that's aligned with what matters most to you, and finding contentment and fulfillment in the process. So take the time to reflect on your values and priorities, and start living the life you truly want to live.

29: Setting Goals for a Fulfilling Life

Life is a journey that can be filled with twists and turns, obstacles and challenges, as well as moments of joy and happiness. Without a clear destination, it can be easy to get lost in the chaos of modern life and feel like you're just going through the motions. That's why it's essential to set goals and create a roadmap for your life. When you have a clear direction, you can focus your energy and take purposeful action towards achieving your dreams. In this chapter, we will explore how to set meaningful goals that align with your values, passions, and purpose and help you lead a fulfilling life.

Before we dive into the nitty-gritty of goal setting, it's essential to understand why it matters. Goals provide a sense of direction, motivation, and purpose. When you have something to work towards, you're more likely to stay focused and persevere through challenges. Goals also help you prioritize your time and resources, ensuring that you're spending your energy on things that matter to you. Additionally, setting and achieving goals can boost your self-confidence and sense of accomplishment, which can have a positive impact on your mental health and well-being.

The first step in setting meaningful goals is to identify your values, passions, and purpose. What matters most to you? What activities do you enjoy? What motivates and inspires you? These questions can help you get clear on what you want to achieve and why it matters to you. When your goals align with your values and passions, you're more likely to stay committed and motivated, even when things get tough.

Next, it's important to set SMART goals. SMART is an acronym that stands for Specific, Measurable, Achievable, Relevant, and Time-bound. Specific goals are clear and concise, so you know exactly what you're working towards. Measurable goals have a specific metric for success, such as a deadline or a specific outcome. Achievable goals are realistic and within your control to accomplish. Relevant goals align with your values and purpose, so you feel a sense of connection to them. Time-bound goals have a specific deadline, so you stay accountable and motivated.

To illustrate how to set SMART goals, let's say your goal is to start a business. A specific goal might be to launch an online store selling handmade candles. A measurable goal might be to make $10,000 in sales within the first six months. An achievable goal might be to start with a small inventory and grow as demand increases. A relevant goal might be to create a product that aligns with your values, such as using eco-friendly materials. A time-bound goal might be to launch the online store by the end of next month.

Once you've set your goals, it's important to break them down into smaller, manageable steps. This makes it easier to stay focused and take consistent action towards achieving your goals. For example, if your goal is to run a marathon, you might break it down into smaller goals, such as running a 5k, 10k, and half-marathon before tackling the full marathon. Breaking your goals down into smaller steps can also help you track your progress and celebrate your accomplishments along the way.

Another essential aspect of goal setting is to stay flexible and adjust your goals as needed. Life is unpredictable, and sometimes circumstances change. If you encounter unexpected obstacles or find that your goals are no longer aligned with your values and passions, it's okay to pivot and adjust your goals. It's better to stay open-minded and adaptable than to get stuck in a rigid plan that no longer serves you.

To stay motivated and on track, it can be helpful to visualize your goals and imagine yourself achieving them. Visualization is a powerful tool that can help you stay focused and motivated, even when faced with challenges. Take some time to imagine what your life will look like when you achieve your goals. What will you feel? What will you see? What will you hear? Use all of your senses to create a vivid mental image of your future self, living the life you've always wanted. Then, use this vision to inspire and motivate you to take action towards your goals.

In addition to visualization, it's important to stay accountable and seek support when needed. Find a friend, family member, or mentor who can hold you accountable and provide encouragement and guidance along the way. Joining a support group or hiring a coach can also be helpful, especially if you're struggling with motivation or need help overcoming obstacles.

Finally, it's important to celebrate your accomplishments and give yourself credit for the hard work you've done.

29: SETTING GOALS FOR A FULFILLING LIFE

Achieving your goals takes effort, dedication, and persever-ance, and you deserve to feel proud of yourself for what you've accomplished. Take some time to reflect on your pro-gress and celebrate your wins, no matter how small they may seem.

In summary, setting meaningful goals is an essential com-ponent of leading a fulfilling life. By identifying your values, passions, and purpose and setting SMART goals that align with them, you can stay focused, motivated, and purposeful as you navigate the challenges and opportunities of modern life. By breaking your goals down into smaller, manageable steps, staying flexible, visualizing your success, staying ac-countable, and celebrating your accomplishments, you can achieve your dreams and unlock your true potential. Re-member, your goals are your roadmap to a fulfilling life, so take the time to set them intentionally and pursue them with passion and purpose.

30: Strategies for Time Management and Productivity

In today's fast-paced world, time management and productivity are crucial to achieving success and maintaining a sense of inner peace. With so many distractions and demands on our time, it's easy to feel overwhelmed and unproductive. However, there are proven strategies and techniques that can help you manage your time more effectively, increase your productivity, and ultimately find contentment and serenity in your daily life.

The first step in improving your time management and productivity is to understand the importance of setting priorities. It's essential to identify the tasks that are most important and require the most attention, and then allocate your time accordingly. This can be done by creating a to-do list or a schedule that outlines your daily tasks and goals. By doing this, you'll be able to stay focused and on track throughout the day, and avoid getting sidetracked by less important tasks or distractions.

Another important strategy for time management and productivity is to learn to say no. Many of us struggle with the fear of missing out or the desire to please others, and as a result, we often take on too many commitments and re-sponsibilities. However, this can lead to overwhelm and burnout, ultimately decreasing our productivity and sense of well-being. By learning to say no to requests and invita-tions that don't align with our priorities or values, we can free up more time and energy for the things that truly mat-ter.

In addition to setting priorities and learning to say no, there are several other techniques that can help us manage our time more effectively and increase our productivity. One of these is the Pomodoro Technique, which involves breaking down work into short, focused intervals of 25 minutes, fol-lowed by a brief break. This technique can help us stay fo-cused and avoid distractions, while also preventing burnout and fatigue.

Another helpful strategy is to establish a morning routine that sets the tone for the rest of the day. This can include activities such as meditation, exercise, or journaling, which can help us center ourselves and cultivate a sense of inner peace and focus. By starting our day with intention and pur-pose, we can be more productive and effective in our daily tasks.

Additionally, it's important to take breaks throughout the day to recharge and replenish our energy. This can involve taking a short walk, engaging in a mindfulness practice, or simply stepping away from our work for a few minutes. By taking regular breaks, we can avoid burnout and increase our overall productivity and effectiveness.

Finally, it's important to cultivate a positive mindset and focus on progress rather than perfection. Many of us struggle with feelings of self-doubt and perfectionism, which can lead to procrastination and decreased productivity. By shifting our focus to progress and growth, we can stay motivated and focused on achieving our goals, rather than getting bogged down by self-criticism and negativity.

Overall, time management and productivity are essential skills for achieving lasting serenity and fulfillment in today's fast-paced world. By setting priorities, learning to say no, using effective techniques like the Pomodoro Technique, establishing a morning routine, taking regular breaks, and cultivating a positive mindset, we can unlock our true potential and achieve success and contentment in all areas of our lives.

31: Balancing Work and Life for Inner Peace

Balancing work and life can be a challenging task, especially in today's fast-paced world where the line between work and personal life is becoming increasingly blurred. Many people find themselves struggling to maintain a healthy work-life balance, often leading to stress, anxiety, and burnout. However, achieving a balanced lifestyle is not impossible, and in fact, it is essential for your overall wellbeing and inner peace. In this chapter, we will explore the importance of balancing work and life, and provide you with practical tips and strategies to help you achieve this balance.

Why is Balancing Work and Life Important?

Achieving a balanced lifestyle is crucial for your physical, mental, and emotional wellbeing. When you are constantly working without taking breaks, you risk burning out and suffering from stress-related illnesses. On the other hand, neglecting work can result in financial insecurity and a lack of fulfillment. By balancing work and life, you can improve your overall quality of life, and achieve a sense of inner peace and contentment.

31: BALANCING WORK AND LIFE FOR INNER PEACE

Tips for Balancing Work and Life

Set Boundaries

Setting boundaries is essential when it comes to achieving a balanced lifestyle. You need to define your work hours and stick to them, allowing yourself time to focus on other areas of your life, such as family, hobbies, and self-care. If you find yourself working overtime, try to prioritize your tasks and delegate responsibilities where possible. It's also important to avoid checking work emails or taking work calls outside of your working hours, as this can disrupt your personal life and lead to burnout.

Prioritize Self-Care

Taking care of yourself is crucial for achieving inner peace and maintaining a healthy work-life balance. Make sure you are getting enough sleep, eating a healthy diet, and exercising regularly. You can also practice self-care activities such as meditation, yoga, or reading a book, to help you unwind and relax after a long day at work.

Create a Schedule

Creating a schedule can help you manage your time more effectively, and ensure you are dedicating enough time to both work and personal life. Use a planner or calendar to schedule your tasks and activities, including work deadlines, appointments, and leisure time. Make sure to include breaks and time for self-care, as this will help you avoid burnout and maintain a healthy work-life balance.

Learn to Say No

Saying no can be difficult, especially if you want to please others or fear missing out on opportunities. However, learning to say no is essential for achieving a balanced lifestyle. If you are already overwhelmed with work, it's okay to say no to additional tasks or responsibilities. Similarly, if you feel like your personal life is being compromised, it's okay to decline invitations or commitments that don't align with your priorities.

Stay Connected

Maintaining positive relationships with family and friends is crucial for achieving inner peace and balance. Make sure to spend quality time with loved ones, and stay connected through regular communication and activities. You can also consider joining social clubs or groups that align with your interests, as this can help you form new connections and enrich your personal life.

Find Fulfillment in Your Work

Finding fulfillment in your work is crucial for achieving inner peace and contentment. If you are not satisfied with your job, it can lead to stress and burnout. Try to find meaning in your work, and focus on the positive aspects, such as learning new skills, making a difference, or building relationships with colleagues. If you are unable to find fulfillment in your current job, consider exploring other career options or pursuing hobbies and interests outside of work.

Conclusion

Achieving a balanced lifestyle is essential for your physical, mental, and emotional wellbeing, and can help you achieve a sense of inner peace and contentment. By setting boundaries, prioritizing self-care, creating a schedule, learning to say no, staying connected, and finding fulfillment in your work, you can achieve a healthy work-life balance and improve your overall quality of life. Remember, achieving a balanced lifestyle is not a one-time event, but an ongoing process that requires effort and commitment. By incorporating these tips and strategies into your daily life, you can transform your life, find fulfillment in the chaos of modern life, and achieve lasting serenity and contentment.

One important aspect of achieving a balanced lifestyle is to manage your time effectively. Time management is a crucial skill that can help you prioritize your tasks, meet deadlines, and achieve your goals. By managing your time effectively, you can also create space for leisure activities, hobbies, and personal growth. Here are some time management tips that can help you achieve a balanced lifestyle:

Create a To-Do List

Creating a to-do list can help you prioritize your tasks and ensure you are focusing on the most important ones. Make a list of your daily, weekly, and monthly tasks, and organize them by priority. Make sure to include both work-related and personal tasks, as this will help you maintain a balanced lifestyle.

Use a Calendar or Planner

Using a calendar or planner can help you stay organized

and manage your time effectively. Use it to schedule your tasks, appointments, and leisure activities, and make sure to allocate enough time for each one. You can also use your calendar or planner to track your progress and evaluate your performance.

Avoid Procrastination

Procrastination is a common time management problem that can lead to stress and anxiety. To avoid procrastination, break down large tasks into smaller ones and tackle them one at a time. Set deadlines for each task and hold yourself accountable for meeting them. You can also try using a timer to help you stay focused and avoid distractions.

Take Breaks

Taking breaks is essential for maintaining your productivity and avoiding burnout. Make sure to take short breaks throughout the day to rest your mind and recharge your energy. You can also schedule longer breaks, such as a weekend getaway or a vacation, to help you relax and unwind.

Learn to Delegate

Delegating tasks can help you save time and focus on the most important ones. Identify tasks that can be delegated to others, such as administrative tasks, and assign them to colleagues or assistants. This will free up your time and allow you to focus on tasks that require your expertise.

In conclusion, achieving a balanced lifestyle is essential for your overall wellbeing and inner peace. By setting boundaries, prioritizing self-care, creating a schedule, learning to say no, staying connected, finding fulfillment in your work, and managing your time effectively, you can achieve a healthy work-life balance and transform your life. Remember, achieving a balanced lifestyle is an ongoing process that requires effort and commitment. By incorporating these tips and strategies into your daily life, you can achieve lasting serenity and contentment, even in the chaos of modern life.

32: The Power of Gratitude and Giving Back

In the midst of the chaos and busyness of modern life, it can be easy to get caught up in our own worries and concerns, and forget about the blessings we have in our lives. It's important to take a step back, slow down, and cultivate an attitude of gratitude.

Gratitude is the practice of acknowledging the good things in our lives, big and small, and recognizing that there is always something to be thankful for. When we focus on what we have, rather than what we lack, we feel happier and more content. This positive outlook can help us cope with stress, anxiety, and other challenges.

One way to cultivate gratitude is to keep a gratitude journal. Each day, write down three things you are thankful for. They can be as simple as a sunny day, a good cup of coffee, or a kind word from a friend. By focusing on the positive, we can train our minds to see the good in every situation.

Another powerful way to cultivate gratitude is to give back to others. When we help others, we not only make a positive impact on their lives, but we also feel good about ourselves.

Giving back can take many forms, from volunteering at a local charity, to donating money or goods to those in need.

Volunteering is a great way to give back and can be a rewarding experience. There are countless opportunities to volunteer in your community, from serving meals at a homeless shelter, to tutoring children, to helping out at a local animal shelter. By giving your time and energy to a good cause, you can make a difference in the lives of others and feel a sense of purpose and fulfillment.

Donating money or goods is another way to give back. There are many organizations that rely on donations to carry out their work, from disaster relief agencies to environmental groups. Consider donating to a cause that is important to you, or participating in a fundraiser to help raise money for a worthy cause.

In addition to giving back, practicing gratitude can also help us become more mindful and present in our daily lives. When we are grateful for what we have, we are less likely to take things for granted and more likely to appreciate the small moments of joy in our lives.

Another way to cultivate gratitude is to focus on the people in our lives who have made a positive impact. Take the time to thank a friend or family member who has been there for you, or write a letter of appreciation to a teacher or mentor who has made a difference in your life. By expressing our gratitude to others, we not only make them feel valued and appreciated, but we also strengthen our own sense of connection and community.

It's important to remember that cultivating gratitude and giving back are not one-time activities, but ongoing practices. By making these habits a part of our daily lives, we can build a foundation of inner peace and contentment that will sustain us through the ups and downs of life.

In conclusion, the power of gratitude and giving back cannot be overstated. By cultivating an attitude of gratitude and giving back to others, we can transform our lives and find lasting serenity and fulfillment. So take a moment to appreciate the good things in your life, and consider how you can give back to those around you. You'll be amazed at how much of a difference it can make.

33: Incorporating Serenity into Your Daily Routine

Achieving serenity and contentment can be a challenging process, especially in the midst of the chaos of modern life. With busy schedules, work demands, and personal obligations, it can be difficult to find the time and space to cultivate a sense of inner peace. However, by incorporating serenity into your daily routine, you can begin to create a more harmonious and fulfilling life.

In this chapter, we will explore some practical strategies for incorporating serenity into your daily routine. We will discuss how to create a peaceful environment, develop mindful practices, and establish positive habits that promote inner peace and contentment. Whether you're a busy professional, a stay-at-home parent, or a student, these tips will help you cultivate serenity and tranquility in your daily life.

Creating a Peaceful Environment

The environment we live in plays a significant role in our mental and emotional well-being. A cluttered, chaotic space can contribute to stress and anxiety, while a clean and organized environment can promote a sense of calm and relaxation. Here are some ways you can create a peaceful environment in your home or workspace:

Declutter: Take some time to go through your belongings and get rid of anything you no longer need or use. A clutter-free space can reduce stress and help you feel more in control.

Simplify: Try to keep your décor and furnishings simple and uncluttered. Use neutral colors and natural materials to create a calming atmosphere.

Bring in nature: Incorporate plants or natural elements into your space, such as a vase of fresh flowers, a small indoor garden, or a natural wood table. Being in nature has been shown to reduce stress and improve mental health.

Use calming scents: Light candles or diffuse essential oils to create a soothing atmosphere. Lavender, chamomile, and bergamot are known for their calming properties.

Reduce noise: Minimize noise and distractions by using earplugs or noise-cancelling headphones. If you're working from home, consider creating a designated workspace that is separate from the rest of your living space.

Developing Mindful Practices

Mindfulness is a powerful tool for promoting serenity and contentment. By being fully present in the moment, we can reduce stress and anxiety and cultivate a sense of calm and peace. Here are some ways you can develop mindful practices in your daily routine:

Start your day with meditation: Take a few minutes each morning to sit quietly and focus on your breath. This can help you set the tone for the day ahead and cultivate a sense of calm and focus.

Practice yoga: Yoga is a great way to combine movement with mindfulness. Practicing yoga can help you improve your physical health while also promoting mental and emotional well-being.

Take mindful breaks: Throughout the day, take a few moments to pause and breathe deeply. This can help you reduce stress and regain focus.

Eat mindfully: When you eat, take the time to savor each

bite and fully experience the flavors and textures of your food. This can help you cultivate a sense of gratitude and appreciation for the simple pleasures in life.

Practice gratitude: Take a few moments each day to reflect on the things you are grateful for. This can help you shift your focus from negative thoughts to positive ones and cultivate a sense of contentment and appreciation.

Establishing Positive Habits

Our habits and routines play a significant role in our overall well-being. By establishing positive habits, we can promote inner peace and contentment and reduce stress and anxiety. Here are some habits you can incorporate into your daily routine:

Exercise: Regular exercise is essential for both physical and mental health. Make it a habit to exercise for at least 30 minutes each day, whether that means going for a walk, hitting the gym, or doing a home workout.

Prioritize self-care: Make self-care a priority in your daily routine. This could mean taking a relaxing bath, reading a book, or practicing a hobby you enjoy.

Set boundaries: Learn to say no to things that don't align with your values or priorities. This can help you reduce stress and create space for the things that truly matter.

Practice time management: Use a planner or calendar to stay organized and manage your time effectively. This can help you avoid feeling overwhelmed or overburdened.

Disconnect from technology: Take breaks from technology and social media. This can help you reduce stress and cultivate a sense of presence and mindfulness in your daily life.

Connect with loved ones: Make time to connect with friends and family members. Social support is essential for mental and emotional well-being.

Practice compassion: Cultivate compassion for yourself and others. This can help you reduce stress and promote a sense of interconnectedness and empathy.

By incorporating these strategies into your daily routine, you can begin to cultivate a sense of serenity and contentment in your life. Remember that the process of achieving

33: INCORPORATING SERENITY INTO YOUR DAILY ROUTINE

inner peace is an ongoing journey, and it requires patience, self-compassion, and a commitment to self-improvement. With time and practice, you can learn to navigate the chaos of modern life with grace and tranquility, and find fulfillment in the present moment.

34: Overcoming Obstacles and Challenges

Life is full of challenges and obstacles that can cause stress, anxiety, and negative thoughts. No matter how hard we try to avoid them, obstacles and challenges are inevitable, and we must learn how to overcome them. In this chapter, we will explore some of the most common obstacles and challenges that people face and provide practical tips and strategies to help you overcome them.

Fear

Fear is one of the most significant obstacles that prevent people from achieving their goals and living a fulfilling life. Fear can manifest in many different forms, such as fear of failure, fear of success, fear of the unknown, and fear of rejection. Overcoming fear is essential to achieving inner peace and contentment. Here are some tips to help you overcome fear:

Acknowledge your fears: The first step to overcoming fear is acknowledging that you have them. Write down all your fears and try to understand where they come from.

Confront your fears: Once you have acknowledged your fears, the next step is to confront them. Face your fears head-on and try to understand why you are afraid. This will help you develop a plan to overcome them.

Take small steps: It's essential to take small steps to overcome your fears. Set small goals and work towards achieving them. This will help you build confidence and overcome your fears gradually.

Practice mindfulness: Mindfulness can help you overcome fear by allowing you to observe your thoughts and feelings without judgment. This will help you become more aware of your fears and allow you to respond to them in a more constructive way.

Seek support: Don't be afraid to seek support from friends, family, or a professional if you need it. Talking to someone can help you gain a new perspective and provide you with the support you need to overcome your fears.

Stress

Stress is another significant obstacle that can prevent us from achieving our goals and living a fulfilling life. Stress can have a significant impact on our physical and mental health, and it's essential to learn how to manage it. Here are some tips to help you overcome stress:

Identify your stress triggers: The first step to managing stress is identifying your stress triggers. Make a list of the things that stress you out and try to understand why they do.

Practice relaxation techniques: Relaxation techniques such as deep breathing, meditation, and yoga can help you manage stress. These practices can help you reduce stress levels and promote relaxation.

Exercise regularly: Exercise is an excellent way to manage stress. Physical activity can help reduce stress levels and release endorphins, which can help improve your mood.

Set boundaries: It's essential to set boundaries and prioritize self-care to manage stress. Say no to things that cause you stress and prioritize the things that bring you joy.

Seek support: Don't be afraid to seek support from friends, family, or a professional if you need it. Talking to someone can help you gain a new perspective and provide you with the support you need to manage your stress.

Negative Thoughts

Negative thoughts are another significant obstacle that can prevent us from achieving inner peace and contentment. Negative thoughts can create a vicious cycle of self-doubt and low self-esteem, and it's essential to learn how to manage them. Here are some tips to help you overcome negative thoughts:

Identify your negative thoughts: The first step to managing negative thoughts is identifying them. Become aware of your negative self-talk and try to understand where it comes from.

Challenge your negative thoughts: Once you have identified your negative thoughts, the next step is to challenge them. Ask yourself if your negative thoughts are accurate and if there is any evidence to support them.

Practice positive self-talk: Replace negative self-talk with positive affirmations. Use phrases such as "I am capable," "I am worthy," and "I can do this." Repeat these affirmations to yourself regularly.

Surround yourself with positivity: Surround yourself with positive people, and engage in activities that make you happy. This will help you cultivate a positive mindset and reduce negative thoughts.

Seek support: Don't be afraid to seek support from friends, family, or a professional if you need it. Talking to someone can help you gain a new perspective and provide you with the support you need to overcome negative thoughts.

Relationships

Relationships can be both a source of joy and a significant obstacle to inner peace and contentment. Building healthy relationships requires effort and commitment, and it's essential to learn how to navigate the challenges that come with them. Here are some tips to help you overcome relationship challenges:

Communicate effectively: Effective communication is the key to building healthy relationships. Be honest and open with your loved ones and try to listen actively to their needs and concerns.

Set boundaries: It's essential to set boundaries and prioritize your needs in relationships. Say no to things that don't align with your values or cause you stress.

Practice forgiveness: Forgiveness is essential to building healthy relationships. Learn to forgive others and yourself for mistakes and misunderstandings.

Seek support: Don't be afraid to seek support from friends, family, or a professional if you need it. Talking to someone can help you gain a new perspective and provide you with the support you need to overcome relationship challenges.

Self-Care

Self-care is essential to achieving inner peace and contentment. Taking care of yourself physically, mentally, and emotionally is crucial to living a fulfilling life. Here are some tips to help you practice self-care:

Prioritize rest: Rest is crucial to physical and mental health. Make sure to get enough sleep and take breaks when you need them.

Practice mindfulness: Mindfulness can help you become more aware of your thoughts and feelings and respond to them in a more constructive way. Practice mindfulness meditation or incorporate mindfulness into your daily activities.

Engage in activities you enjoy: Engage in activities that bring you joy, whether it's reading, painting, or going for a walk. These activities can help reduce stress levels and promote relaxation.

Eat well and exercise: A healthy diet and regular exercise are essential to physical and mental health. Make sure to eat a balanced diet and engage in physical activity regularly.

Seek support: Don't be afraid to seek support from friends, family, or a professional if you need it. Talking to someone can help you gain a new perspective and provide you with the support you need to practice self-care.

In conclusion, overcoming obstacles and challenges is essential to achieving inner peace and contentment. By acknowledging and confronting our fears, managing stress, overcoming negative thoughts, building healthy relationships, and practicing self-care, we can transform our lives and unlock our true potential. Remember that it's okay to seek support from others and that the journey to inner peace is ongoing. With patience, commitment, and a willingness to learn and grow, you can overcome any obstacle and achieve lasting serenity.

35: Celebrating Your Progress and Successes

As we journey through life, it is important to pause and take stock of our progress and successes. Celebrating our achievements, no matter how small they may seem, is a powerful way to build confidence, boost our morale, and cultivate a sense of contentment and serenity. In this chapter, we will explore the art of celebrating progress and successes and how it can transform our lives.

Why Celebrating Progress and Successes Matters

The road to success and contentment is often a long and winding one, and it is easy to get bogged down by setbacks and challenges. Celebrating our progress and successes, however small they may seem, can be a powerful tool to help us stay motivated and inspired.

Celebrating our progress and successes allows us to acknowledge the hard work, effort, and determination that we have put in to achieve our goals. It also helps us to recognize the positive impact that our efforts have had on our lives and the lives of those around us.

35: CELEBRATING YOUR PROGRESS AND SUCCESSES

By celebrating our progress and successes, we create a positive feedback loop that reinforces our good habits and encourages us to continue working towards our goals. This, in turn, can help us to develop a more positive and optimistic outlook on life, which is crucial for achieving lasting contentment and serenity.

How to Celebrate Progress and Successes

Now that we understand why celebrating progress and successes is important, let's explore some practical ways to celebrate our achievements:

Take Stock of Your Progress

Before you can celebrate your progress and successes, you need to be aware of them. Take some time to reflect on the progress you have made towards your goals. This could involve journaling, creating a mind map, or simply taking a quiet moment to think about what you have accomplished.

As you reflect on your progress, try to focus on the positive changes that you have made. Think about the challenges you have overcome, the skills you have developed, and the lessons you have learned. Remember, even small steps forward are worth celebrating.

Share Your Successes with Others

Sharing your successes with others can be a powerful way to celebrate your achievements and reinforce your positive habits. This could involve telling a friend or family member about your progress, posting about it on social media, or even writing a blog post or article about your experiences.

Sharing your successes with others not only allows you to celebrate your achievements, but it can also inspire and motivate others to work towards their own goals.

Treat Yourself

Treating yourself is a classic way to celebrate your achievements, but it can be easy to fall into the trap of rewarding yourself with unhealthy habits, such as overeating or overspending. Instead, try to find healthy and meaningful ways to treat yourself.

For example, you could buy yourself a new book, take a relaxing bath, or indulge in a hobby that you enjoy. The key is to choose something that makes you feel good and reinforces your positive habits and values.

Set New Goals

Setting new goals is a powerful way to celebrate your progress and successes while also staying motivated and inspired. As you reflect on your achievements, think about what you want to accomplish next.

This could involve setting new goals that build on your existing successes, or it could involve branching out into new areas of interest. Whatever your goals may be, make sure they are challenging yet achievable and align with your values and priorities.

Practice Gratitude

Practicing gratitude is a powerful way to cultivate a sense of contentment and serenity in your life. Take some time each day to reflect on the things you are grateful for, whether it be your health, your relationships, or simply the beauty of nature.

By focusing on the positive aspects of your life, you can build a stronger sense of appreciation and fulfillment, which can help you to weather the storms of life with greater ease and resilience.

Celebrate the Successes of Others

Finally, it is important to remember that celebrating progress and successes is not just about our own achievements. Celebrating the successes of others can be just as powerful, both for them and for ourselves.

When we celebrate the successes of others, we reinforce a sense of community and connection, and we help to build a more positive and supportive environment for everyone. This, in turn, can help us to feel more fulfilled and content in our own lives.

Conclusion

Celebrating progress and successes is a powerful tool for building confidence, boosting morale, and cultivating a sense of contentment and serenity in our lives. By taking stock of our progress, sharing our successes with others, treating ourselves, setting new goals, practicing gratitude, and celebrating the successes of others, we can create a positive feedback loop that reinforces our positive habits and values.

Remember, celebrating progress and successes is not just about achieving our goals; it is about acknowledging the hard work, effort, and determination that we have put in to get there. By taking the time to celebrate our achievements, no matter how small they may seem, we can build a stronger sense of appreciation and fulfillment in our lives, which is crucial for achieving lasting contentment and serenity.

36: Embracing a Life of Serenity and Fulfillment

As human beings, we all have an innate desire to experience happiness, contentment, and fulfillment in our lives. Unfortunately, in today's fast-paced world, many of us find ourselves constantly rushing from one task to another, with little time to pause and reflect on what truly matters. We become so caught up in the hustle and bustle of modern life that we forget to take care of ourselves and our inner well-being.

The good news is that it doesn't have to be this way. By embracing a life of serenity and fulfillment, you can learn to navigate the challenges of modern life with grace and ease, while still achieving your goals and pursuing your dreams.

In this chapter, we'll explore the power of inner peace and how you can cultivate it in your own life. From mindful practices to positive habits, you'll learn how to overcome stress, anxiety, and negative thoughts, and unlock your true potential with the ultimate self-help resource.

Understanding the Importance of Inner Peace

36: EMBRACING A LIFE OF SERENITY AND FULFILL-MENT

Before we dive into the practical steps you can take to cultivate inner peace and fulfillment, it's important to understand why this is such a crucial component of a happy and healthy life.

At its core, inner peace is a state of being in which you feel calm, centered, and content with yourself and your life. When you're at peace with yourself and the world around you, you're able to handle challenges and setbacks with greater resilience and grace. You're less likely to become overwhelmed by stress, anxiety, or negative emotions, and you're better equipped to maintain healthy relationships with others.

Inner peace is not just a nice-to-have luxury; it's a fundamental aspect of human well-being. Research has shown that people who experience a sense of inner peace are less likely to suffer from mental health disorders such as depression and anxiety, and they're more likely to live longer, healthier lives.

With this in mind, let's take a closer look at some of the practical steps you can take to cultivate inner peace and find fulfillment in your life.

36: EMBRACING A LIFE OF SERENITY AND FULFILL-MENT

Practical Steps for Cultivating Inner Peace and Fulfillment

Practice Mindfulness

One of the most effective ways to cultivate inner peace is through the practice of mindfulness. Mindfulness is the art of being fully present in the moment, without judgment or distraction.

When you're mindful, you're able to focus your attention on the present moment, rather than getting caught up in worries about the future or regrets about the past. This can be incredibly liberating, as it allows you to let go of the mental chatter that can so often create stress and anxiety.

There are many different mindfulness techniques you can try, such as meditation, deep breathing, or simply taking a few minutes to focus on your senses and the world around you. The key is to find a practice that works for you and to make it a regular part of your routine.

Cultivate Positive Habits

Another important step in cultivating inner peace and fulfillment is to develop positive habits that support your well-being. This might include things like exercising regularly, eating a healthy diet, getting enough sleep, and spending time in nature.

When you prioritize your physical health, you're better able to cope with the stresses and challenges of daily life. You'll have more energy, greater mental clarity, and a stronger sense of resilience and optimism.

Practice Self-Care

In addition to prioritizing your physical health, it's also important to practice self-care on a deeper level. This might involve taking time to do things you enjoy, such as reading, painting, or spending time with loved ones. It might also mean setting boundaries with others, learning to say no when you need to, and taking time for quiet reflection and introspection.

When you prioritize your own well-being in this way, you're better able to show up fully in your life and relationships, without becoming overwhelmed or burnt out.

Practice Gratitude

36: EMBRACING A LIFE OF SERENITY AND FULFILL-MENT

Another powerful way to cultivate inner peace and fulfill-ment is through the practice of gratitude. When you focus on the good things in your life, rather than dwelling on the negative, you're able to cultivate a sense of joy and content-ment.

Try starting a gratitude journal, in which you write down three things you're grateful for each day. This simple prac-tice can help you to reframe your perspective and focus on the positive aspects of your life.

Let Go of Negative Thoughts and Emotions

One of the biggest obstacles to inner peace and fulfillment is negative thoughts and emotions. Whether it's fear, anger, or self-doubt, these feelings can create a lot of stress and anxi-ety in your life.

Learning to let go of negative thoughts and emotions is an essential part of cultivating inner peace. This might involve practicing mindfulness to become more aware of your thoughts and emotions, and learning to observe them without judgment or attachment.

It might also involve learning to reframe negative thoughts into more positive ones, or engaging in activities that help you to release pent-up emotions, such as journaling, exercise, or talking to a trusted friend or therapist.

Connect with Others

Finally, it's important to remember that human connection is a fundamental part of our well-being. Cultivating strong, healthy relationships with others can help to create a sense of meaning and purpose in your life, and provide a source of support and comfort during difficult times.

Make an effort to connect with others on a regular basis, whether it's through socializing with friends, joining a community group, or volunteering for a cause you care about. These connections can help you to feel more fulfilled and supported, and can be an important source of inner peace and contentment.

Conclusion

Cultivating inner peace and fulfillment is not always easy, but it's an essential component of a happy and healthy life.

36: EMBRACING A LIFE OF SERENITY AND FULFILL- MENT

By practicing mindfulness, cultivating positive habits, prioritizing self-care, practicing gratitude, letting go of negative thoughts and emotions, and connecting with others, you can learn to navigate the challenges of modern life with grace and ease, and find lasting serenity and fulfillment. Remember that this is an ongoing process, and that it takes time and practice to develop these habits and skills. But with patience, persistence, and a commitment to your own well-being, you can transform your life and experience the peace and contentment you deserve.

Thank You

As we reach the end of this book, I want to say thanks for reading this book.

I want to get this information out to as many people as possible. If you found this book helpful, I would greatly appreciate you leaving me a review. This helps others find the book as well.

Disclaimer

This document is geared towards providing exact and reliable information in regards to the topic and issue covered. The publication is sold on the idea that the publisher is not required to render an accounting, officially permitted, or otherwise, qualified services. If advice is necessary, legal, financial, medical or professional, a practiced individual in the profession should be ordered.

This information is not presented by a financial or medical practitioner and is for entertainment, educational and informational purposes only. The content is not intended as a substitute for professional medical advice, diagnosis, or treatment. Always seek the advice of your physician or other qualified health care provider with any questions you may have regarding a medical condition. Never disregard professional medical advice or delay in seeking it because of something you have read.

The information provided herein is stated to be truthful and consistent, in that any liability, in terms of inattention or otherwise, by any usage or abuse of any policies, processes, or directions contained within is the solitary and utter responsibility of the recipient reader. Under no circumstances

DISCLAIMER

will any legal responsibility or blame be held against the publisher for any reparation, damages, or monetary loss due to the information herein, either directly or indirectly.

www.ingramcontent.com/pod-product-compliance
Lightning Source LLC
Chambersburg PA
CBHW060513130626
46553CB00002B/472